A CHILD CENTRED
EYFS

A CHILD CENTRED EYFS

AARON BRADBURY
RUTH SWAILES

1 Oliver's Yard
55 City Road
London EC1Y 1SP

2455 Teller Road
Thousand Oaks
California 91320

Unit No 323-333, Third Floor, F-Block
International Trade Tower
Nehru Place, New Delhi – 110 019

8 Marina View Suite 43-053
Asia Square Tower 1
Singapore 018960

Editor: Amy Thornton
Senior project editor: Chris Marke
Cover design: Wendy Scott
Typeset by: C&M Digitals (P) Ltd, Chennai, India
Printed and bound by CPI Group (UK) Ltd, Croydon, CR0 4YY

Library of Congress Control Number: 2024944292

British Library Cataloguing in Publication data

A catalogue record for this book is available from the British Library

ISBN 978-1-5296-7322-7
ISBN 978-1-5296-7321-0 (pbk)

CONTENTS

ABOUT THE AUTHORS

Aaron Bradbury is the Principal Lecturer for Early Childhood, Childhood and Early Years at Nottingham Trent University. Aaron is a member of the Coalition for Early Years on the Birth to Five Matters Non-Statutory Guidance for the EYFS and chaired and wrote the Equalities and Inclusion section with colleagues in the sector. Aaron is the Co-Chair of the Early Childhood Studies Degrees Network.

Aaron is a published author on early childhood related literature. He sits on many national and early childhood groups and is also a consultant on many aspects of early years and child development. Aaron has a passion for making the voice of the child, nurturing through a diverse lens and pioneers of early childhood the foreground of practice.

Ruth Swailes is an award-winning consultant with more than 30 years' experience in primary education, including primary headship and many senior leadership roles. Ruth has worked as a School Improvement Advisor, Early Years consultant and moderator in several local authorities, supporting leaders and teachers to improve outcomes for pupils. Passionate about primary education, particularly Early Years, Ruth has taught from Nursery to Y6. Ruth is the lead author and developer of the Oxford International Early Years curriculum for children aged 2-6 years.

INTRODUCTION

It's been an interesting couple of years, both professionally and personally, since the publication of our first book, *Early Childhood Theories Today*.

Aaron has become Dr Aaron Bradbury and Ruth became a widow. Both of us became infamous after allegedly critiquing the DfE, leading to us being deemed 'unsuitable' to speak at a DfE-funded conference because we are not afraid to speak up when we feel something isn't right for children.

Speaking out is tricky, but through our professional roles we both see the impact of inappropriate expectations on adults and children in the sector. We are currently in the midst of a recruitment and retention crisis. When we speak to practitioners we're repeatedly told about their frustration when they're being asked to do things that they know may not be right for the children in their care in the name of ambition, or because someone who doesn't work directly with the children thinks this is best practice, or perceives this is what Ofsted will expect to see.

With 50 years combined experience in the sector, we're all too familiar with the external pressures those working with young children face, and the number of people who've never actually worked with young children who think they know best how it should be done. Over the last two years, following the pandemic and with an increased Ofsted and DfE focus on Early Years, it's now more difficult than ever to navigate your way through all the rhetoric, opinion and research and get to the heart of what matters: *children*. What's truly heartening and inspiring is that despite the increasing pressure to conform and push pedagogy more suited to older children into the Early Years we have the privilege of working with amazing practitioners who manage to be creatively compliant and do the right thing for children, in spite of all the challenges they face.

While Aaron has been busy writing his PhD and spreading the word about *nurture*, Ruth has been writing the *Oxford International Early Years Curriculum*. On our travels we've met so many people who want to do the right thing for their children, know what they'd like to do, and are seeking reassurance and research to support them in their thinking.

That's where this book comes in. It is not a prescriptive guide. You are the professional. Nobody knows the children you work with better than you and their families. You won't find a series of chapters telling you how to teach. What you will find is some research, provocations, case studies, questions and reflections based on our work over the last few decades with thousands of practitioners and based on our own experience of working with young children, providers, settings and schools. Some things you will probably agree with, some things you probably won't. That's a good thing. A reflective practitioner who thinks for themselves, who looks through their own unique lens and thinks about the community and children they serve is a far better practitioner than one who reads a book and follows the script blindly. We want you to challenge us, we all need to be challenged, it's how we grow!

In the following pages we hope you find much to support and challenge your thinking. We hope to give you affirmation and professional confidence, and the fire in your belly to stand up for what's right for young children, even when it's scary, because we're standing with you. None of us should ever forget that the reason we all do the jobs we do, whatever they are in the Early Years sector, is to make things better for children, and they should be at the heart of all our decision-making.

Thanks to all who have supported us through difficult times over the last two years; there are too many friends and colleagues to mention but every single message of support has meant the world to us both, and we can never thank you enough. Ruth's thanks go to Charlie and Hannah, my girls who make me proud every day and who have kept me going with coffee, advice and support when I wanted to give up, and, of course, to Pete who may not be with me physically any more but is always the voice in my head saying, 'I'm so proud of you' and reminding me to keep speaking out for those who can't speak for themselves. Aaron's thanks go to my husband Gary who believes in me every day, and my colleagues within the Childhood team at Nottingham Trent University. I could not ask for more genuine colleagues than those I work with, *thank you*. Further thanks go to our publishers and editors for their patience and encouragement and to all the people we work with who inspire us every day.

Aaron and Ruth

1

BUILDING THE VISION

Play is the highest expression of human development in childhood for it alone is the free expression of what is in a child's soul.

Friedrich Froebel, Early Education, 2021

Early childhood is a time for building a positive self-identity, a time when children need to explore who they are, and a time for understanding and making sense of their place in the world.

Dr Sharon Colilles, Froebel Trust, n.d.

INTRODUCTION

This chapter comes to you at a time when the Early Years is going through a significant change, both in terms of the curriculum and the belief from professionals that child development has to have a place when developing our children for learning. We want to focus on the core aspects of the Early Years Foundation Stage (EYFS), reflecting on the pioneering work of Froebel and why play should be at the forefront of Early Years practices. With the implementation of the EYFS in recent years, much debate has arisen regarding what constitutes effective practice in the early childhood sector and the methods of implementing this application to children's learning. As Early Years practitioners, we know that child-centred practice is what matters. Despite the pressures for more 'school-like' learning in the Early Years, professionals and practitioners in the field continue to advocate for child-led best practice in settings.

This book is a toolkit for all those working with children on how to develop and implement a child-centred curriculum for delivery of the EYFS. A curriculum that is research-informed and based on what we know about children's development and learning; a curriculum that ensures children have the time and space to explore and develop the fundamental building blocks of early development. Since the EYFS was first introduced in 2008, it has been amended on a number of occasions, with revisions such as changes to the Early Learning Goals (ELGs) and a greater emphasis on the safety of children and school readiness. As of 2018, the EYFS underwent more changes aimed at reducing teacher workloads and improving children's outcomes – especially in language, literacy, and mathematics – with the expectations that these changes would be implemented by 2020. However, this was pushed back due to the Covid-19 pandemic, and we saw much of this implementation in 2021.

The purpose of this book is to help those who are implementing the EYFS to maintain the ethos of balancing theory and practice to develop a critical approach to key issues and to keep the child at the centre of our practices. By incorporating pedagogical elements, such as case studies, reflections and discussion points, we expand on questioning our approaches and to think holistically without losing our focus on practice. As argued by Palaiologu (2021), there remains some scepticism around the implementation of the EYFS, especially with the growing emphasis on 'school readiness'. As a result of the statutory nature of the EYFS assessment profile, the inspection of settings and the emphasis on school readiness, it is important to emphasise that this is not as much a demonstration of a culture of frameworks and guidance as a symptom of a central, prescribed and standardised curriculum.

We, as professionals who are working with children and families, must stop thinking that there is a standardised process and approach, as demonstrated in the chapters of this book, and become united and understand that our pedagogy and practices play a crucial role in developing a curriculum that is child-centred and free from the white noise of policy-makers and the documents that we have come to see as attempts to standardise approaches within the EYFS. We have the opportunity to re-evaluate our roles, recognise that we still have autonomy within our daily practices, and focus on the reasons why we do certain things and the benefits that they provide. A central focus on the child is at the core of bringing the EYFS back to the child.

WHAT IS A CHILD-CENTRED PRACTICE?

The term 'child-centred practice' is used to describe a specific approach to early childhood education and care (ECEC) pedagogy, but it is a multifaceted term influenced by both cultural and historical considerations. Over 40 different uses of the term 'child-centred practice' are cited by Chung and Walsh (2000) in their overview of understandings of child-centred practice over history. Based on their analysis, child-centredness can be grouped under three core ideals: the child at the centre of the world; a developmental view of the child at the centre of learning; and a progressive view of the child at the centre of learning. In spite of the fact that being child-centred appears to have its origins in the works of Froebel, Dewey, Rousseau, Montessori and Vygotsky (Chung and Walsh, 2000), the mix of theorists illustrates the term's evolving history, where romantic ideas of the natural curiosity of children have been combined with understandings of child development, accompanied by more democratic conceptions. According to Rhedding-Jones (2005), child-centred care is a hybrid of developmental psychology with cultural and sociological theories.

Taking a child-centred approach means:

- ensuring that all aspects of the service are designed to meet the individual needs and abilities of each child;
- ensuring that all children have the same opportunity to access and participate in all aspects of the programme;
- adapting and tailoring activities to meet the unique needs of each child;
- participating in decision-making with the child, their family and their support team;
- ensuring that the child's voice and preferences are taken into consideration;
- all participants are encouraged to reflect and provide feedback.

INVOLVING ALL CHILDREN IN DECISION-MAKING FOR A CHILD-CENTRED APPROACH

ASK THE CHILD TO SUGGEST IDEAS

Their unique viewpoints and ideas may contribute to the discussion. Seeing their contributions and preferences reflected in the programme will make them feel respected and valued. As a result, they will be engaged and motivated.

For example, ask the children to nominate their favourite activities for a market-style day. Plan activities for children with complex disabilities based on pictures or a list of activities they are interested in.

OBSERVE ALL CHILDREN, WHAT ARE THEY TELLING US THROUGH PLAY?

All children, including those with complex disabilities, may have difficulty identifying or expressing what they enjoy about the service you provide. By watching their behaviour and interactions and what they gravitate towards and choose to engage with, you will better understand their preferences.

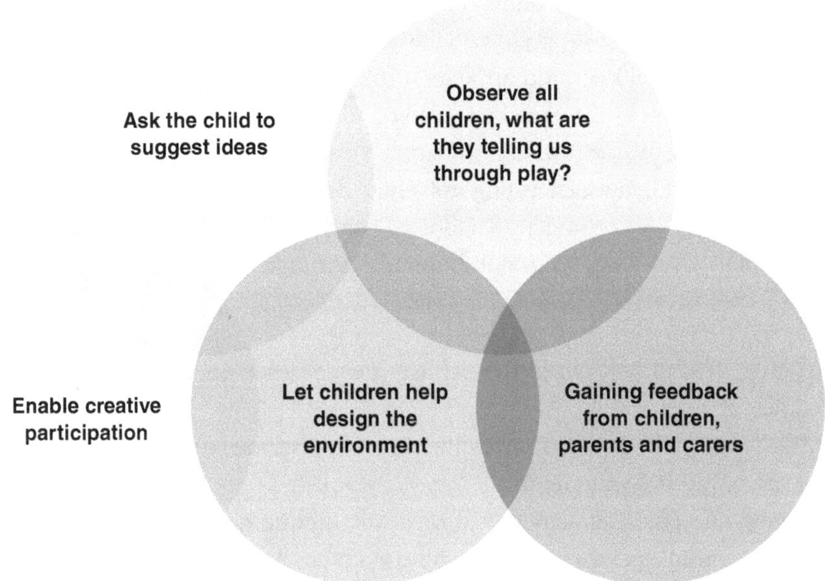

Figure 1.1 Children's involvement in decision-making

As an example, create different sensory stations for self-directed play and observe which activities the child enjoys participating in. During unstructured playtimes, see what the child gravitates towards.

ENABLE CREATIVE PARTICIPATION

Every child will experience participation in an activity differently. Depending on the child, some may prefer to lead, others may join in for just a part of an activity, and others may choose to observe rather than participate.

You may wish to provide children with a variety of opportunities to participate in an activity, and some children may wish to simply observe and comment. It is okay for children to participate in what they feel comfortable doing, which means that you are tailoring the activity and environment to meet the needs of the children. When the child is ready and confident to participate, an invitation must always be available.

LET CHILDREN HELP DESIGN THE ENVIRONMENT

They will feel more ownership over the space since it is 'theirs' and was designed according to their preferences.

For example, children may want to decorate the walls with their own art or hang handprints with their names on them. Consult with them regarding the layout of the space.

GET FEEDBACK FROM CHILDREN, PARENTS AND CARERS

The purpose of asking the child for their feedback is to make them feel heard and valued as well as to inform you of any changes that may need to be made.

This can be achieved by making feedback processes fun and using techniques that are suited to the child's communication abilities and preferences. Observing how the children interact with their play and what they are interested in will provide you with some initial feedback. It is important to provide opportunities for parents and caregivers to participate in the feedback process, both formally and informally.

A CHILD-CENTRED EARLY YEARS CURRICULUM TODAY: WHAT ABOUT PLAY?

Children's intellectual and social development, as well as their wellbeing, are impacted by access to high-quality early childhood education (Sylva et al., 2004). As a result of a growing discourse surrounding early childhood education, early childhood programmes are being viewed from a human capital perspective, putting quality outcomes within a broader economic context focusing on what education should accomplish. Children's play is considered to be a foundation for learning and development in early childhood. Despite the assumption that play should contribute to learning outcomes, the place of play within ECEC policy frameworks remains debated (Fesseha and Pyle, 2016; Hunter and Walsh, 2014). However, play is caught between a number of discourses, including freedom, child-initiated play, adult-led play, the role of the adult and determining predetermined learning outcomes. There are many factors to consider when defining play. Cultural–historical factors should be taken into consideration when implementing play within different systems, as demonstrated by Cheng Pui-Wah et al. (2015) in Hong Kong, and Hedges et al. (2018) in New Zealand, Ontario and Brazil. Early childhood educators can support both child-initiated play and adult-driven, playful approaches to learning and teaching through integrative approaches to play and pedagogy (Fleer, 2015).

There is often less child-initiated play as a result of increased demands placed on practitioners, which leads to more adult instructional techniques to respond to targets and the school readiness agenda. As children enter preschool, this pressure increases. Nicholson (2018) refers to the discontinuity from EYFS to Year 1 (formal curriculum), but the political discourse is now driving the expectations of outcomes for children earlier and earlier. During the transition from the EYFS to the first-class year of the National Curriculum (Year 1), *Bold Beginnings* (Ofsted, 2017) highlighted a misalignment of expectations. Hoskins and Smedley

(2019, p. 74) report an increased drive to develop children's academic skills to compete in the PISA tests. PISA is the Organisation for Economic Cooperation and Development (OECD)'s Programme for International Student Assessment that compares the academic achievements of 15-year-olds in core subjects.

The fight to retain play as opposed to educational attainment is a constant threat to the wellbeing and educational outcomes of young children. As a result of the emphasis on ensuring children are ready for school and achieving 'school readiness', a context of academic pressure has been observed within Early Years settings in England. In recent years, ECEC have been the subject of policy reform as part of neoliberal reforms of education systems (Moss and Roberts-Holmes, 2022). Historically, professionals were allowed to work independently, trained in Montessori, Froebel and Steiner philosophies, and permitted to operate without the burden of regulation (Hoskins and Smedley, 2019). There has been a rise in regulation of the Early Years, including the profession and curriculum, in the English educational sector, together with the adoption of accountability measures in this sector within the United Kingdom and worldwide (Bradbury, 2014), in contrast to the situation in the Early Years when there were no laws.

As a result of the EYFS and National Curriculum, there is a narrow and prescriptive vision of how learning and play should take place. It is important to remember that play should be exploratory and adventurous, is complex and requires a deep understanding of child development in addition to years of experience to assess effectively. As a social construct, accountability, evidentiary and political warrants are necessary to drive policy development.

PLAY

> Play is essential for children's development, building their confidence as they learn to explore, relate to others, set their own goals and solve problems. Children learn by leading their own play, and by taking part in play which is guided by adults.
>
> (DfE, 2021b)

Play is a fundamental part of this book. It goes without saying that each chapter will focus on an element of play. It is the right of children to play. There is no doubt that children's right to play is vital to their wellbeing and development, which is why it is included in the UN Convention on the Rights of the Child (1989) (UNICEF, 2019). Throughout the EYFS, children are encouraged to play both indoors and outdoors. Thompson (2024) argues that the past decade has seen important changes in thinking and reflecting critically on approaches to play.

As children play, they can take things they already know and combine them in new ways, thereby deepening their understanding. Through interaction with an open-ended environment and quality resources, or alongside a playful adult, they may build on existing knowledge. It is through the transformation of their knowledge into new connections and applications that children develop mastery of concepts. Skills and knowledge are embedded, ideas and new ways of thinking are explored, creativity is supported, and dispositions are developed. To be able to discuss this with parents, adults must have a deep understanding of how different types of play support children's development and learning. As a result of research, many different types of play have been identified, which has enabled practitioners to better understand the choices children make and how to best support their learning.

It is possible for children to pursue a variety of purposes in sensory play, exploratory play with objects, schematic play, symbolic play, pretend play (alone, with a role or with small world objects), cooperative role play with others, fantasy and superhero play, physical play, rough play, risky play, or digital play. All of these types of play support children's development and learning in different ways, so early childhood providers should ensure that all types of play are available to children. Adults can gain insight into a child's purpose through observing and reflecting on their play. Due to the spontaneous, flexible and unique nature of play, settings may have difficulty supporting and advocating for play. The unique ability of play to reveal children's dispositions to learn is essential for practitioners. As part of supporting meaningful experiences that are inclusive of all families, settings should also understand and respect the individual, cultural approaches to play adopted by each family.

In the Early Years, children not only develop and learn through play; children have the opportunity to learn through first-hand experiences of various kinds in addition to being taught how to do things, having conversations, and participating in activities designed by adults to introduce or practise particular skills. Adult-led activities such as these are not play, but they are most effective when they incorporate some aspects of play in order to engage and motivate children. They should offer children choices, hands-on experiences, connections to their interests and enjoyment.

WHAT DOES THE FRAMEWORK SAY?

We have a government-driven agenda here in England which provides us with a statutory framework. The EYFS Statutory Framework sets standards for the learning, development and welfare of children from birth to age five. As a result of these standards, which must be met by schools and childcare providers, young children will be able to develop and learn safely.

As part of the EYFS Statutory Framework, young children are encouraged to remain safe while learning new skills and developing holistically.

The EYFS framework is designed to provide every child with the best possible start in life with a supportive system that helps them reach their full potential. In the early years of a child's life, they develop and learn rapidly, and their first five years have a significant impact on their future. An important factor in ensuring a positive learning start is having a secure and happy childhood, which typically stems from a loving home environment and high-quality early childhood education.

A framework such as this is essential for guiding children's early education and providing a solid foundation for their future success. A child's educational journey is greatly influenced by the EYFS framework, which sets standards for the early years of learning and development.

The EYFS (DfE, 2023) has identified four main guiding principles for practitioners. These demonstrate the framework's dynamic nature and its ability to adapt and evolve in order to better support the development of children.

- *Recognise every child as unique*: Understanding and acknowledging each child's individuality is crucial. Children, who are always learning, can grow to be resilient, capable, confident and self-assured.
- *Foster positive relationships for independence*: Developing strong and positive relationships is a key part of helping children learn and grow. These relationships encourage them to become more independent and establish a sense of self.
- *Create enabling environments for learning and development*: An environment that supports individual interests and needs significantly enhances children's learning. In such nurturing spaces, adults guide children, enabling them to gradually construct their knowledge and understanding.
- *Celebrate the individual pace and learning*: This principle underlines the fact that children learn and develop at their own pace. The EYFS framework caters to all children, including those with special educational needs and disabilities (SEND). It's designed to ensure every child receives the support they need.

The non-statutory guidance document *Development Matters*, first published by Early Education in 2012, sits alongside the EYFS. By updating this document in 2021, the Department for Education (DfE, 2021a) provides guidance on observing and assessing children in early education, and it can assist practitioners in making summative assessments of individual children, to determine whether they are on the right track with their development.

NON-STATUTORY GUIDANCE FOR THE EARLY YEARS FOUNDATION STAGE

There are many non-statutory documents which form the basis of guidance for the EYFS curriculum. Practitioners are free to choose one which suits their needs or select from a range of guidance. For our book, we wanted to align to one which allows for child-centred practices and places the child at the centre of our daily practices. This guidance is *Birth to 5 Matters: Non-statutory Guidance for the Early Years Foundation Stage* (Early Years Coalition, 2021).

Birth to 5 Matters:
Non-statutory guidance for the
Early Years Foundation Stage

From the Early Years Coalition
www.birthto5matters.org.uk

Figure 1.2 *Birth to 5 Matters: Non-statutory Guidance for the Early Years Foundation Stage*

> Birth to 5 Matters provides comprehensive guidance, drawing on previous guidance for the Early Years Foundation Stage (EYFS) which has been updated in order to reflect recent research, to meet the needs of practitioners, to respond to current issues in society, to meet the needs of children today and to lay a strong foundation for their futures.
>
> (Early Years Coalition, 2021)

The purpose of the guidance is to reaffirm the core principles which recognise the areas shown in Figure 1.3.

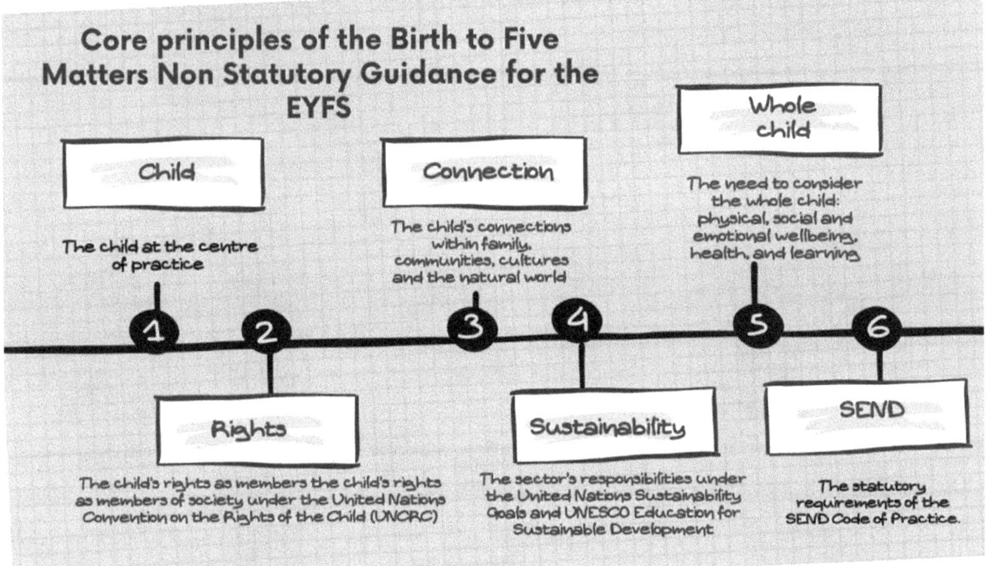

Figure 1.3 Core principles of the *Birth to 5 Matters: Non-statutory Guidance for the Early Years Foundation Stage*

It is the goal of *Birth to 5 Matters* to assist practitioners in all aspects of their statutory obligations within EYFS areas of learning and development and educational programmes, as well as to help children achieve the ELGs. Even though the government has stated that the ELGs are not the curriculum, there is a statutory duty to help children work towards the ELGs. A setting can determine for itself what, when and how to offer experiences and support that will enable children to make progress in their learning and development. It has been observed, in some cases, that the arrangement of strands within *Birth to 5 Matters* differs from that in the ELGs, where a more logical arrangement aligned with the developmental needs of children is used. As a result, practitioners will be able to gain a better understanding of how children develop throughout the EYFS and how they might support children's progress. In the 'Learning for Life: Characteristics of Effective Learning' (Early Years Coalition, 2021, p. 22), the word 'teaching' does not appear since the aforementioned characteristics pertain to the behaviour and disposition of children rather than adults. 'Creating and thinking critically' has been rephrased to 'Thinking creatively and critically' (p. 22), to emphasise the critical thinking skills that are fundamental to the creative process.

It is important to recognise that as Early Years professionals we can make use of many other non-statutory documents. Washwood Heath Nursery School developed its Early Years curriculum by drawing upon many Early Years curriculum guidances to tailor it to the needs of its nursery and children. This includes *Development Matters* (Early Education, 2012), *Birth to 5 Matters* (Early Years Coalition, 2021), *Realising the Ambition* (Education Scotland, 2021), *Development Matters* (DfE, 2021a), International Baccalaureate (n.d.) and the *Oxford International Curriculum for Early Years* (Oxford University Press, 2022).

CASE STUDY 1.1

DR VALERIE DANIEL, EXECUTIVE HEADTEACHER, WASHWOOD HEATH MAINTAINED NURSERY SCHOOL

DEVELOPMENT OF THE EARLY YEARS CURRICULUM

Our curriculum is the central guide in both our schools for us as educators to be able to generate and explore ideas so that every child has access to a rigorous, dynamic learning experience, strengthened by innovative educational approaches, pedagogy and an engaging environment.

We believe that our curriculum should not be static because this is the stage when brain growth is most active in children. A child's brains develops more from birth to five years old than at any other time in life. Research tells us that early brain development has a lasting impact on a child's ability to learn and succeed in school and in later life. So, it is of the utmost importance for us in the Early Years to be clear on what we are doing, as our impact on a child's life will outlive us.

Our curriculum is based primarily on the EYFS (Educational Programmes) as it is the Statutory Curriculum Framework that needs to be adhered to by all Early Years providers. However, we can all build our curriculums differently. In our schools, we debated what our curriculum should look and feel

(Continued)

like, and it is designed to comprise the method, structure and skills needed in a high-quality learning environment. We use the six themes of the International Baccalaureate to structure the EYFS. The International Baccalaureate is a transdisciplinary educational approach that focuses on not compartmentalising learning and is centred on how children construct meaning in the context of real-world experiences. We also work with other educational approaches like Reggio Emilia which strongly supports our creative pedagogies. We ensure that our curriculum is culturally responsive so that equity and inclusivity are promoted in our teaching and learning strategies. This helps to support our children's sense of identity in a positive way and provide scope to explore and engage with the culture of other people meaningfully and naturally. We leaned heavily on researching and co-constructing to build our curriculum using *Development Matters, Birth to 5 Matters* and *Realising the Ambition* (the Scottish non-statutory guidance) to formulate our own flexible, unique, dynamic curriculum. I was recently asked how we could manage so many intricate aspects – well, our curriculum was built piece by piece on a foundation of strong leadership, ensuring vision, values, ethos and philosophy and it is grounded in praxis and andragogy to nurture agency and autonomy in our practitioners and the children in our care.

LAYING THE FOUNDATIONS FOR THE HIGHEST QUALITY PROVISION: PRINCIPLES OF THE EARLY YEARS FOUNDATION STAGE

Birth to 5 Matters, which shows how these principles apply to children in the EYFS, is based on the four principles of the EYFS (see Figure 1.4). The development of each child is unique, and it is not a linear or automatic process. Each child must have opportunities to interact with positive individuals and be exposed to enabling environments that encourage engagement and recognise their strengths. As children develop their agency and curiosity for learning, they will interact in different ways with other people and the world around them. To understand who children are and how to best support their development, we must understand these different ways of knowing about the world.

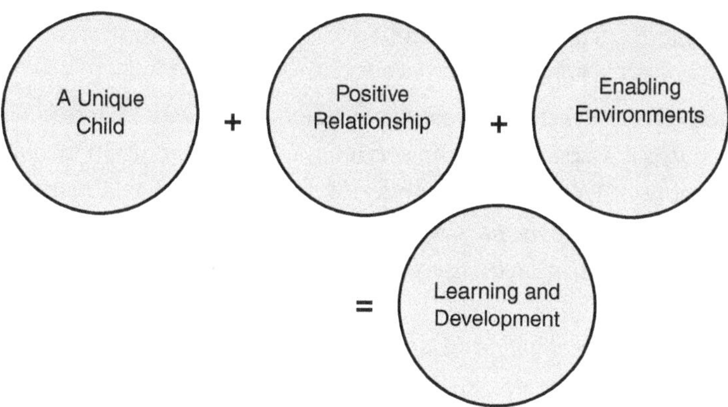

Figure 1.4 Creating an EYFS where children feel like they belong

KEY POINTS OF THE CHAPTER

1. What is a child-centred curriculum? We look at why we adopt this phrase and what it means for the professional and the child.
2. Play needs to be central to the needs of the child's development.
3. To be child-centred, the rights of the child need to be at the forefront of practice, values and approaches.
4. For an effective Early Years curriculum to flourish, Early Years professionals need to be more holistic when planning their approaches to learning.
5. We focus on the core principles of the EYFS and making sure that child development is fundamental to building curriculum knowledge.

REFERENCES

Bradbury, A. (2014) Early childhood assessment: Observation, teacher 'knowledge' and the production of attainment data in Early Years settings. *Comparative Education*, 50(3), 322–339.

Cheng Pui-Wah, D., Reunamo, J., Cooper, P., Liu, K. and Keang-ieng Vong, P. (2015) Children's agentive orientations in play-based and academically focused preschools in Hong Kong. *Early Child Development and Care*, 185(11–12), 1828–1844.

Chung, S. and Walsh, D.J. (2000) Unpacking child-centredness: A history of meanings. *Journal of Curriculum Studies*, 32(2), 215–234.

Department for Education (DfE) (2021a) *Development Matters: Non-Statutory Curriculum Guidance for the Early Years Foundation Stage*. Available at: https://assets.publishing.service.gov.uk/media/64e6002a20ae890014f26cbc/DfE_Development_Matters_Report_Sep2023.pdf [Accessed 1 February 2024].

DfE (2021b) *Early Years Foundation Stage Profile. EYFS Reforms Early Adopter Version*. Available at: https://assets.publishing.service.gov.uk/media/5f68b0eb8fa8f50763644e5e/Early_adopter_schools_EYFS_profile_handbook.pdf [Accessed 1 January 2024].

DfE (2023) *Statutory Framework for the Early Years Foundation Stage*. Available at: www.gov.uk/government/publications/early-years-foundation-stage-framework--2 [Accessed 1 January 2024].

Early Education (2012) *Development Matters in the Early Years Foundation Stage (EYFS)*. Available at: https://dera.ioe.ac.uk/id/eprint/14042/7/development%20matters%20in%20the%20early%20years%20foundation%20stage_Redacted.pdf [Accessed 12 December 2023].

Early Education (2021) *Who was Friedrich Froebel (1782–1852)*. Available at: https://early-education.org.uk/friedrich-froebel/#:~:text=He%20believed%20that%20%E2%80%9Cplay%20is,through%20direct%20experience%20with%20it [Accessed 1 January 2024].

Early Years Coalition (2021) *Birth to 5 Matters Non-statutory Guidance to the Early Years Foundation Stage*. Available at: https://birthto5matters.org.uk/wp-content/uploads/2021/03/Birthto5Matters-download.pdf [Accessed 1 January 2024].

Education Scotland (2021) *Realising the Ambition, Being Me: National Practice Guidance for Early Years in Scotland*. Available at: https://education.gov.scot/media/3bjpr3wa/realisingtheambition.pdf [Accessed 1 January 2024].

Fesseha, E. and Pyle, A. (2016) Conceptualising play-based learning from kindergarten teachers' perspectives. *International Journal of Early Years Education*, 24(3), 61–37.

Fleer, M. (2015) Pedagogical positioning in play: Teachers being inside and outside of children's imaginary play. *Early Child Development and Care*, 185(11–12), 1801–1814.

Froebel Trust (n.d.) *The Power of Play and Inclusion*. Available at: www.froebel.org.uk/about-us/the-power-of-play/play-and-inclusion#:~:text=Froebel%20described%20play%20as%20%22the,and%20interpret%20ideas%20about%20ethnicity [Accessed 1 January 2024].

Hedges, H., Peterson-Stagg, S. and Wajskop, G. (2018) Modes of play in early childhood curricular documents in Brazil, New Zealand and Ontario. *International Journal of Play*, 7(1), 11–26.

Hoskins, K. and Smedley, S. (2019) Protecting and extending Froebelian principles in practice: Exploring the importance of learning through play. *Journal of Early Childhood Research*, 17(2), 73–87.

Hunter, T. and Walsh, G. (2014) From policy to practice? The reality of play in primary school classes in Northern Ireland. *International Journal of Early Years Education*, 22(1), 19–36.

International Baccalaureate (n.d.) *IB Primary Years Programme (PYP) Early Years*. Available at: www.ibo.org/primary-years-programme-in-the-early-years/ [Accessed 1 November 2023].

Moss, P. and Roberts-Holmes, G. (2022) Now is the time! Confronting neo-liberalism in early childhood. *Contemporary Issues in Early Childhood*, 23(1), 96–99.

Nicholson, P.M. (2018). Play-based pedagogy under threat? A small-scale study of teachers' and pupils' perceptions of pedagogical discontinuity in the transition to primary school. *Education 3–13. BG Research Online*. Available at: https://bgro.repository.guildhe.ac.uk/id/eprint/324/1/Nicholson_play%20based%20pedagogy_2018.pdf [Accessed 1 January 2024].

Ofsted (2017) *Bold Beginnings: The Reception Curriculum in a Sample of Good and Outstanding Primary Schools*. Manchester: Crown Copyright.

Oxford University Press (2022) *Oxford International Curriculum for Early Years: A Play-based, Student-focused Curriculum that Puts the Child at the Centre*. Available at: https://global.oup.com/education/content/primary/series/oxford-international-primary/early-years/?region=uk [Accessed 1 December 2023].

Palaiologou, I. (2021) *The Early Years Foundation Stage: Theory and Practice* (4th edn). London: Sage.

Rhedding-Jones, J. (2005) Decentering Anglo-American curricular power in early childhood education: Learning, culture, and 'child development' in higher education coursework. *Journal of Curriculum Theorizing*, 21(3), 133.

Sylva, K., Melhuish, E., Sammons, P., Siraj-Blatchford, I. and Taggart, B. (2004) *The Effective Provision of Pre-school Education (EPPE) Project: Final Report: A Longitudinal Study Funded by the DfES 1997–2004*. Institute of Education, University of London/Department for Education and Skills/Sure Start.

Thompson, P. (2024) Play in early childhood. In D. Fitzgerald and H. Maconochie, *Early Childhood Studies: A Students Guide* (Chapter 9). London: Sage.

United Nations Children's Fund (UNICEF) (2019) *A Summary of the UN Convention on the Rights of the Child*. Available at: www.unicef.org.uk/rights-respecting-schools/wp-content/uploads/sites/4/2017/01/Summary-of-the-UNCRC.pdf [Accessed 1 November 2023].

2

WHAT CHILD DEVELOPMENT TELLS US: WHAT CHILDREN REALLY NEED

It is not that man must develop in order to work, but that man must work in order to develop. The work of the hand is the expression of psychic growth.

Maria Montessori, 1946

INTRODUCTION

Even though general patterns of development from pre-birth to early childhood can be helpful, each child's development unfolds differently and is influenced by their own uniqueness and the environment. This is aligned with the *Birth to 5 Matters: Non-Statutory Guidance for the Early Years Foundation Stage* (Early Years Coalition, 2021) which states 'The complex differences for each child mean the pathways toward maturity should be seen more as dancing around a ballroom than climbing a ladder' (p. 18). From conception to early childhood, an individual's growth, development and learning are intrinsically linked in complex ways. It is important to note that the experiences a child has in their early years have a significant effect on their future development, as both development and learning are built upon the experiences of the early years.

THERE ARE MANY FACTORS THAT CONTRIBUTE TO THE DEVELOPMENT OF AN INDIVIDUAL

Throughout life, the body, mind, abilities and behaviour of infants, children and adults develop and become more complex. As the child grows so do cognition, memory, attention, language and communication, feelings and relationships, as well as sensory-motor skills. Development is often considered as a combination of different aspects; it cannot really be compartmentalised since one aspect very often influences the development of another. The many factors that influence a child's development must be considered in the context of the whole child.

There is a growing interest among early childhood professionals in learning more about the developing brain and how we nurture children's development, seeking to better understand children's needs. Nurturing the brain and focusing on child development holistically have recently become obvious ways to facilitate early childhood education. In Early Years, nurture development is concerned with offering a balance of opportunities for children to help with healthy brain development, to maintain a focus on the child's learning capabilities and to support each child to reach their full potential. Research tells us that nurturing an emotional relationship is the primary function needed for intellectual and social growth (Bradbury and Swailes, 2022).

STARTING WITH BRAIN DEVELOPMENT

A child's brain continues to develop from birth; by the age of five, 90 per cent of brain growth has occured. At this age, the brain has developed more than at any other time in the child's development. Learning and success in life are strongly influenced by the development of the child's brain in their early years. It is the experiences a child has during their first few years of life, both positive and negative, that help shape how their brain develops.

Baby brains are approximately one-quarter the size of an average human brain at birth. In the first year, the brain doubles in size. At the age of three, the brain is about 80 per cent of its adult size and by the age of five it has nearly reached its full size.

In a child's body, the brain serves as a command centre. In a newborn baby, all of their brain cells (neurons) are present. Brain function is primarily determined by the connections between cells. As a result of the connections in the brain, we are able to move, think, communicate, connect and perform most functions with our bodies. The early years are crucial for the development of these connections. Every second, more than a million new neural connections (synapses) are formed.

It is important to note that different areas of the brain are occupied by different functions, and these areas respond to different abilities, such as language, emotions and movement. As the brain develops, connections eventually link together in a variety of complex ways, and the brain develops by itself. In the early years, a child's brain has the best opportunity to develop the connections needed to develop many higher-level abilities such as motivation, self-regulation, problem solving and communication. It is more important during the early years of a child's life to establish essential brain connections than later on in life.

REFLECTION 2.1

WHY IS IT IMPORTANT THAT WE KNOW THIS?

Experiences, relationships and interactions shape brain development at a very rapid pace, especially between birth and two years old, with effects lasting throughout a person's lifetime.

WHAT DOES THIS LOOK LIKE IN PRACTICE?

Examine the learning environment and resources: are they conducive to babies and children engaging using all their senses? Each brain processes information, responds, makes decisions, thinks and solves problems in a unique way.

Consider whether you provide learning experiences that challenge the brain's ability to respond actively, to assimilate information from a variety of sources and to generate new possibilities and ideas.

Are the activities and resources designed to provide the children with enough stimulation and interest while also encouraging them to solve problems on their own?

PHYSICAL DEVELOPMENT

As part of the EYFS and other early childhood curricula, physical development is considered to be a vital aspect of a child's development. It is not necessary to make it complicated when planning for physical development. Everyday activities can incorporate it. Movement and self-care play a major role in physical development in the early years. Development of the physical body is described by Devlin (2023) as the movement of one's whole body, primarily through gross and large motor movements, such as running and jumping. Aspects of physical development include fine motor skills, or small motor movements, such as pinching, making marks and threading.

Several studies have shown that young children are driven to move, and that moving and handling objects are among the most natural learning opportunities in early childhood. Richardson et al. (2023) argue that being out in the natural environment is beneficial for young children's physical, social, emotional and cognitive development. The research also demonstrates how being out in nature supports early language development. In addition to learning through movement, children are also learning how to move. Children benefit from movement by developing their gross motor skills. In the early years, there are three gross motor movements that are important (see Figure 2.1).

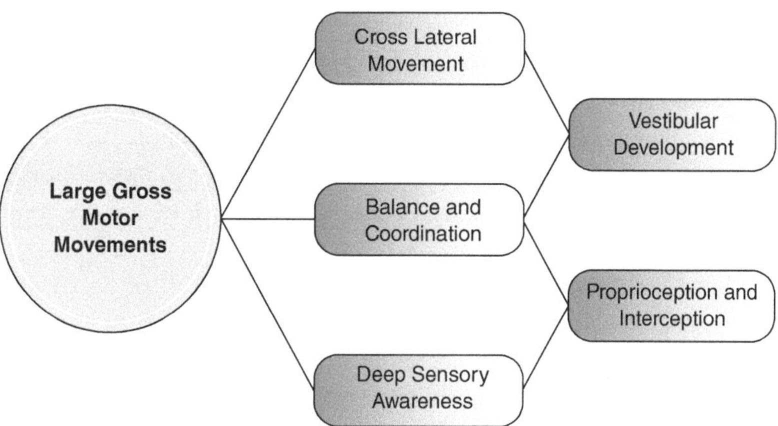

Figure 2.1 Large gross motor movements for young children

Cross-lateral movement: When both sides of the body are used simultaneously, movement crosses the midline of the body. Performing cross-lateral movements such as running, walking and pedalling facilitates the development of cross-lateral movement. We can benefit from helping our hands, arms, legs, feet and eyes coordinate and work together. By exposing children to these movements, they will be able to establish stronger connections between their left and right brains. Children will be able to sequence their thoughts and words more effectively if they are capable of handling more complex sensory input. Speech, communication and early writing skills will be coordinated and sequenced as a result.

Balance and coordination: Balance and coordination are supported by the vestibular system. These movements provide information to the inner ear. During head movement, the vestibular system is stimulated by movement fluid in the inner ear. Jumping, whirling, spinning and other types of movement are common among children. A child who is exposed to these types of movements is more likely to be able to self-regulate their bodies and pay greater attention for a longer period of time.

Deep sensory awareness: It is important to understand where our bodies are in space as well as where the parts of our bodies are without having to search for them. Consequently, the body and mind are in close coordination. Furthermore, it provides children with an opportunity to become familiar with the amount of force required to lift an object (Devlin, 2023).

EMOTIONAL AND SOCIAL DEVELOPMENT

Practising emotional and social development in early childhood is an integral part of everyday skills of working with children. Young children are able to explore their surroundings freely when they feel emotionally and physically secure. It is important for children to be able to interact with adults and other children, to gain a sense of identity by understanding and being confident in themselves as individuals. Providing a strong, positive, secure environment in which relationships can develop is the most important aspect of emotional and social development. It is imperative that children are nurtured by adults who are responsive and supportive. Children develop independence in a safe, stable and welcoming environment provided by caring adults.

As Bradbury and Grimmer (2024) demonstrate, the approach of developing children's emotional and social development should be the bedrock of early child development. When an Early Years professional thinks about nurturing children, this implies caring for them over time or as they grow. By nurturing curiosity, kindness, or creativity in our children, we are helping them develop these virtues or foster these dispositions. The act of nurturing someone involves caring for them deeply and assisting them in their growth and development. As a result, the primary purpose of our early childhood programme is to nurture children. Taking care of children goes hand in hand with loving them. Nurturing is essential to loving a child, since real love is active and strives to achieve the best outcome for the other person.

REFLECTION 2.2

PERSONAL, SOCIAL AND EMOTIONAL DEVELOPMENT AND THE EYFS

The development of personal, social and emotional development (PSED) does not take place in isolation, and it is essential that you provide positive feedback to your children and model appropriate behaviour. To support children's PSED, you are the best resource in your setting.

There are many areas in which children can feel secure. An effective key person approach is crucial in creating a nurturing environment and tuning in to the child. As a further recommendation, the following contribute to social and emotional development:

- *routine*: it is important to establish routines for children as they begin to understand the structures of the day;
- *feelings*: it is important for children to learn to recognise their feelings as well as to learn the appropriate words to use when expressing them;
- *role modelling*: by acting as a role model and praising children who demonstrate positive behaviours, you can reinforce the behaviours you prefer;
- *communication*: pay attention to both verbal and non-verbal communication.

THEORIES OF CHILD DEVELOPMENT

Understanding these theories will aid in the development of developmentally appropriate practices when reflecting on your own childcare practices. As a result, you will be able to better understand certain behaviours and how children learn. One of these is *stage theory*. It is important to recognise that not all children develop in the same way and at the same stage as each other. Therefore, stage theory has a place, but understanding the child's uniqueness also needs to be central to understanding where children are at developmentally.

Children's cognitive, emotional, social, physical and behavioural development is studied in child development theory. Children's development and learning are better understood through theories. Our teaching methods are based on their predictions of future needs of the unique child, which includes certain behaviours. A variety of child development theories exist, each with its own set of assumptions and beliefs. There are some theories that are based on scientific evidence and others that are not. For example, Piaget's Theory of Cognitive Development, Kohlberg's Moral Stages, Bronfenbrenner, Bourdieu, Montessori, Vygotsky's Zone of Proximal Development and Lev Vygotsky's Theory of Social Learning are some of the theories. Bradbury and Swailes (2022) argue that early childhood pioneers and theorists are the backbone of our practices in working with children 0–8 years and families. We continually hear about how we need to link theory to practice as it allows us to continue to put the child at the centre of what we do. The early childhood pioneers and theorists are undoubtably influencing our thinking, as well as our practices, when it comes to child development.

URIE BRONFENBRENNER: ECOLOGICAL SYSTEMS THEORY

According to Bronfenbrenner, the environment in which a child grows up has a profound impact on their development and should be taken into account (Grimmer, 2022). He offers a theoretical perspective on how humans are affected by an interconnected system containing many parts, or 'environments for human development' (Bronfenbrenner, 1979, p. 8). In his theory, he places the child at the centre and discusses the processes and conditions that have an impact on them at different times. Children are influenced by many factors, such as their family, home environment, or nursery setting, which may have a direct or indirect effect on them.

His theory is presented as a model with concentric rings, sometimes referred to as circles of influence, with the child at the centre. Different systems are located outward from the centre, each of which has a different degree of influence on the child. Children's lives are examined in terms of the processes and conditions that influence them at various times (Bronfenbrenner and Ceci, 1994). The parts were each given a name, and they have been described as layers in an onion (Buchan, 2013), nested systems, or Russian dolls (Rosa and Tudge, 1979; Bronfenbrenner, 1999; Bronfenbrenner, 2013). Rather than simply experiencing their environment, the child is viewed as an active individual who can influence and alter their own environment (Manoli and Papadopoulou, 2012), rather than simply experiencing it as a passive participant (Plomin and Bergeman, 1991). By creating a 'supportive ecology around a child' (Brendtro, 2006, p. 165), the aim is to view the child holistically, taking into account all influences on the individual child.

JEAN PIAGET: COGNITIVE THEORY, SENSORIMOTOR STAGE

Piaget developed a stage theory called the *sensorimotor stage*. This relates to cognitive development of a child which relates to a lot of what we see within Early Years practice today. Piaget's theory is based on stages, where each stage builds upon the last. He believes that infants are on the sensorimotor stage. He goes on to explore inborn reflexes which include:

- *rooting*: turning their heads towards something that touches their cheek;
- *sucking*: the tendency to suck at things that touch their lips;
- *stepping*: the movement of legs when they are held with their feet touching the floor;
- *object permanence*: the understanding that objects and people exist even when they cannot be seen.

Piaget's theory may be contested. However, the discussion of child development has to come from somewhere. Development is a continual process which is influenced by many start factors. According to *Birth to 5 Matters* (2021), child development refers to the process through which the body, brain, abilities and behaviour of the infant, child and adult become more complex and mature in confidence throughout life. Using the model developed within *Birth to 5 Matters* there are many factors which influence development as shown in Figure 2.2 on page 26.

LEV VYGOTKSY: SOCIO-CULTURAL THEORY

Social interaction plays a crucial role in shaping and enhancing the cognitive development and learning abilities of a child, according to Vygotsky's social development theory. According to this theory (also called Vygotsky's *socio-cultural theory*), learning is a social process rather than an individual exploration. A parent or teacher can play an important role in guiding a child's learning as a more knowledgeable member of the community.

According to Vygotsky's socio-cultural theory, children internalise and learn from the beliefs and attitudes they observe around them. Cultural factors are considered to play a significant role in shaping cognitive development, thus resulting in a variation in cognitive development across cultures. Language is also considered to be the root of all learning by Vygotsky.

ABRAHAM MASLOW: SELF-ACTUALISATION THEORY

In order to develop intellectually, socially, emotionally and physically, basic physical needs must be met, and a sense of security must be established. In 1943, Maslow proposed this theory, which remains highly relevant to this day. According to Maslow, people are instinctively motivated to fulfil certain needs. As soon as one need is met, a person seeks to fulfil the next need (Maslow, 1943).

A child's early experiences can have a profound impact on their growth, development and behaviours. They develop strong communication skills, a curiosity to learn new things and a sense of wellbeing as a result of their positive experiences with peers and adults. A baby's primary caregiver is responsible for all aspects of their life. In order to make sense of the world around them, they require reciprocal relationships and unconditional love and care (Hunt, 2022).

JOHN BOWLBY: ATTACHMENT THEORY

Attachment theory was developed by John Bowlby, a renowned British psychiatrist and psychoanalyst who is considered a pioneer of the field. It has transformed the way we understand early childhood development. Relationships between a child and their primary caregiver have a profound influence on an infant's emotional and social development.

According to Bowlby, infants are biologically wired to form attachments, a mechanism that serves as a survival mechanism. In the early years of a child's life, these attachments are not just transient bonds, but are integral to the development of the child's emotional health and interpersonal relationships throughout their life.

The importance of having a secure and consistent attachment to your primary caregiver is underscored by Bowlby's attachment theory. As a result of disruptions or inconsistencies in these early attachments, Bowlby hypothesised that a range of mental health and behavioural problems could develop as we age.

Historically, mental health issues were often attributed to innate or genetic factors, but this perspective marked a significant shift from those theories. Bowlby's theory emphasises the influence that early childhood experiences have on an individual's life trajectory.

In addition to the concept of individual differences in attachment patterns, Bowlby's theory was further developed by his colleague Mary Ainsworth in her seminal work, *Patterns of Attachment* (1979). In addition to validating Bowlby's theory, Ainsworth's research provided a framework for understanding the different attachment styles – secure, avoidant and anxious –resulting from early caregiver interactions.

We are moving forward with these theories of early childhood development. A child's development can be influenced in many ways by Early Years professionals. In Figure 2.2, these factors are outlined. In the diagram, each area of a child is discussed along with how each interaction can affect the development of that child.

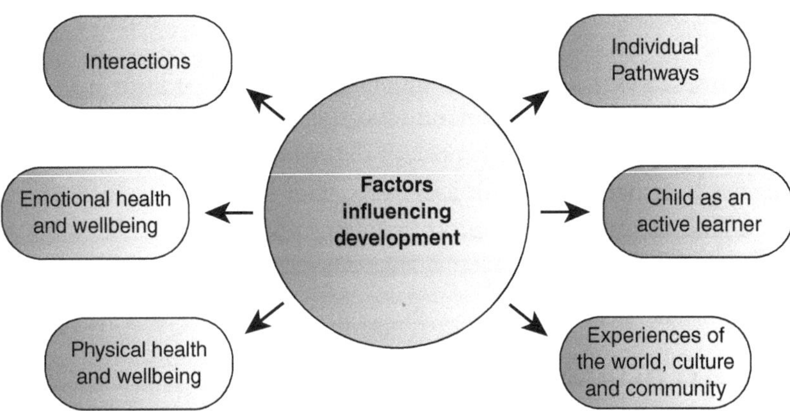

Figure 2.2 Factors influencing child development

REFLECTION 2.3

Using the diagram on page 26 (Figure 2.2) think of ways in which you influence a child's development and then complete Table 2.1; the first factor, Interactions, has been filled in as an example.

Table 2.1 Ways to influence a child's development in practice

Factors influencing development	Adopting practices within my role
Interactions	Every interaction I have with children is an important one. I have focused on reflecting on how I allow children the time to play. Thinking about when I step in and interrupt play, do I do this often, do I interact with the child and ask them questions? Do I model language? ...
Emotional health and wellbeing	
Physical health and wellbeing	
Individual pathways	
Child as an active learner	
Experiences of the world, culture and community	

KEY POINTS OF THE CHAPTER

An early childhood curriculum should focus on child development. As an early childhood educator, it is important to be able to learn and grow from the experience of working with children. It is important for early childhood educators to understand how children can progress with the guidance and assistance of their pedagogical leadership. Understanding child development provides a clear strategy for understanding the child, implementing affective pedagogy, and meeting the needs of the unique abilities of every child. It is important to recognise that child development is constantly evolving and that information and knowledge about this are constantly being developed. It is influenced by research in a number of areas including developmental psychology and cognitive neuroscience, as well as day-to-day practices.

(Continued)

- Being able to work with different children is key to successes of development and achievement within the EYFS.
- Keeping up to date with studies around child development is important; this includes opening your horizons to new and up-and-coming theories.
- It is important not to stretch children too soon. Slow down the expectations and make sure that all planning and activities are age- and stage-appropriate.
- Understand the child, their development and have appropriate expectations, including what the child brings to the table such as their knowledge and skills.

REFERENCES

Ainsworth, M.D.S. (1979) *Patterns of Attachment: A Psychological Study of the Strange Situation*. New York: Psychology Press.

Bradbury, A. and Grimmer, T. (2024) *Love and Nurture in the Early Years*. London: Learning Matters.

Bradbury, A. and Swailes, R. (2022) *Early Childhood Theories Today*. London: Learning Matters.

Brendtro, I. (2006) The vision of Urie Bronfenbrenner: Adults who are crazy about kids. *Reclaiming Children and Youth*, 15(3), 162–166.

Bronfenbrenner, U. (1979) *The Ecology of Human Development: Experiments by Nature and Design*. Cambridge, MA: Harvard University Press.

Bronfenbrenner, U. (1999) Environments in developmental perspective: Theoretical and operational models. In S. Friedman and T. Sachs, *Measuring Environment Across the Lifespan: Emerging Methods and Concepts*. Washington, DC: American Psychological Association Press.

Bronfenbrenner, U. and Ceci, S. (1994) Nature-nurture reconceptualized in developmental perspective: A bioecological model. *Psychological Review*, 101(4), 568–586.

Buchan, T. (2013) *The Social Child: Laying the Foundations of Relationships and Language*. London: Routledge.

Devlin, C. (2023) *Physical Development in the Early Years*. Available at: https://early-education.org.uk/physical-development-early-childhood/ [Accessed 1 February 2024].

Early Years Coalition (2021) *Birth to 5 Matters Non-statutory Guidance to the Early Years Foundation Stage*. Available at: https://birthto5matters.org.uk/wp-content/uploads/2021/03/Birthto5Matters-download.pdf [Accessed 1 January 2024].

Grimmer, T. (2022) Bronfenbrenner. In A. Bradbury and R. Swailes, *Early Childhood Theories Today* (Chapter 2). London: Learning Matters.

Hunt, M. (2022) *Helping Every Child to Thrive in the Early Years: How to Overcome the Effect of Disadvantage*. London: Routledge.

Manoli, P. and Papadopoulou, M. (2012) Graphic organizers as a reading strategy: Research findings and issues. *Creative Education*, 3, 348–356.

Maslow, A.H. (1943) A theory of human motivation. *Psychological Review*, 50(4), 370–396.

Montessori, M. (1946) *The 1946 London Lectures*. Available at: https://montessori150.org/maria-montessori/montessori-books/1946-london-lectures [Accessed 13 June 2024].

Plomin, R. and Bergeman, C. (1991) The nature of nurture: Genetic influence on environment measures. *Behavioural and Brain Sciences*, 14, 373–427.

Richardson, T., Waite, S. Askerlund, P., Almers, E. and Hvit-Lindstrand, S. (2023) How does nature support early language learning? A systemic literature review. *Early Years: An International Research Journal*, 1–28. Available at: https://doi.org/10.1080/09575146.2023.2220978 [Accessed 27 May 2024].

Rosa, E. and Tudge, J. (2013) Urie Bronfenbrenner theory of human development: Its evolution from ecology to bioecology. *Journal of Family Theory and Review*, 5(4), 243–258.

3

THE SEVEN AREAS OF LEARNING: THE EARLY YEARS CURRICULUM

All Areas of Learning are interconnected, demonstrating the holistic nature of young children's development.

Pascal, Bertram and Rouse, 2019

INTRODUCTION

Seven areas of learning and development within the EYFS are set out within the Statutory Framework; these are important for the child to be able to flourish and develop within the Early Years and they are interconnected. The seven areas are used in Early Years settings and by professionals to shape their curriculum and determine what should be taught to aid children's learning and development.

The seven areas are split into two categories:

1. The prime areas

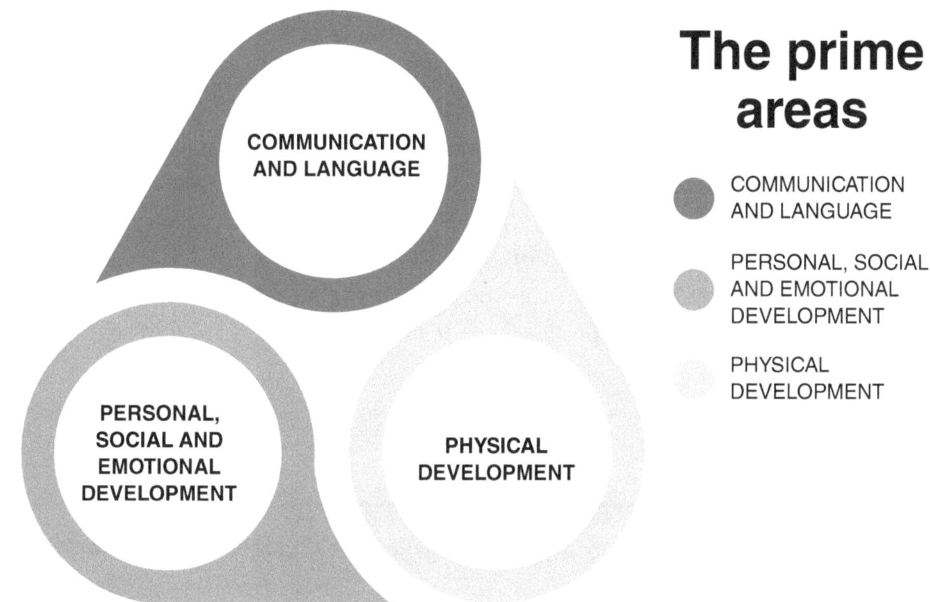

Figure 3.1 The prime areas of development

2. The specific areas

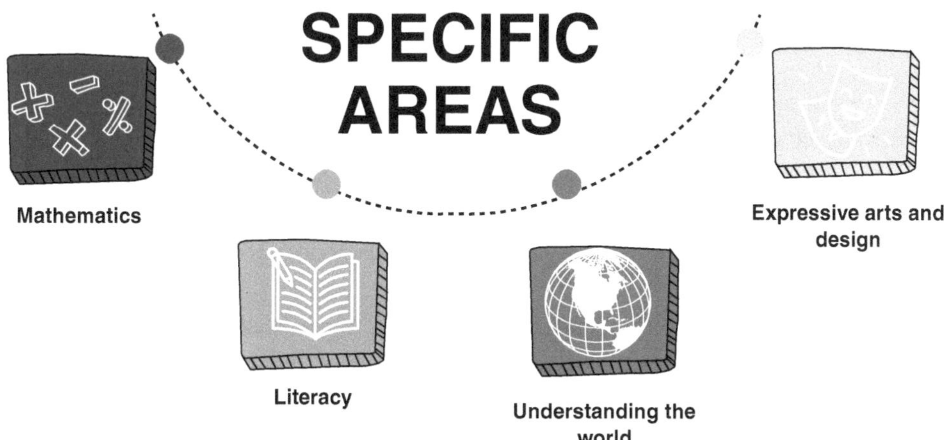

Figure 3.2 The specific areas of development

Within this chapter, we will give a detailed account of the seven areas of the Early Years curriculum, including areas which we feel would be important to maintain a child-centred focus on learning and development. It is also an opportunity to maintain a focus of how to continue this focus within your daily practices. It is important to note that the EYFS Statutory Framework itself is only a skeleton, consisting of an outline of the learning and development requirements and settings will want to build a curriculum based on the educational programmes, to meet the needs of your own unique learners. The document lists the seven areas of learning and development and describes in very broad terms the types of educational experiences and activities that children should be exposed to from birth onward. Additionally, the EYFS lists the ELGs, but they should not be used as a curriculum – only as an assessment at the end of the Reception year. The *Early Years Foundation Stage Profile: 2024 Handbook* (DfE, 2023) reinforces this message. It is vital that practitioners build a curriculum based on the educational programmes if they are to provide a rich experience for the children in their care.

THE PRIME AREAS

The prime areas were added to the curriculum because of the Tickell review in 2011.

> It is when those foundations are not strong that we can see children struggle, finding it difficult to focus, to adapt to routines, and to cooperate with others. Therefore, I recommend that personal, social, and emotional development, communication and language and physical development are identified as prime areas of learning in the EYFS.
>
> (Tickell, 2011)

A prime area serves as a foundation for the development of all future learning. In early childhood development, the three prime areas are the development of: personal, social and emotional skills (PSED); communication and language skills (CL); and physical development (PD). As a result of biological factors, brain connections develop rapidly in the first three years of life and continue throughout early childhood. It is imperative that children's interactions and experiences during their first few years support development in these fundamental areas in order to avoid missing crucial developmental steps later on in life.

Across all areas of development, all three of the prime areas are continuously in action. Children experience and develop a sense of themselves, others' feelings and support each other throughout the day through links of social and emotional development. Children will be engaged in movement and are learning to understand and communicate with others. As stated in the *Birth to 5 Matters* (Early Years Coalition, 2021), children are able to access the world around them and build relationships with others, which, in turn, opens the door across all areas when they learn about a sense of self, movement and communication. Further, it suggests that the prime areas have a strong influence in the specific areas of learning and development.

There is widespread agreement among researchers and practitioners that PSED, CL and PD are closely related and are integral to all other areas of learning and development. These three interdependent areas represent the earliest stages of development, which begin before birth and continue throughout the first few years of life, when the developing brain is at its most predisposed to learning (Tickell, 2011). We believe that PSED is the foundation for learning. As discussed in other chapters, Grimmer (2021) assures us that love and nurture is at the forefront of practice to support the development of empowerment of our children so that they are ready to learn. This is also discussed by Pascal et al. (2019), in the research review called *Getting it Right in the Early Years*, which states that:

> There is evidence to suggest that there should be some modifications to the current EYFS Statutory Framework to give greater prominence to the Characteristics of Effective Teaching and Learning and Personal, Social and Emotional Development to ensure the foundational skills, understandings and knowledge in these areas are securely in place before more advanced, challenging learning is introduced to the children.
>
> (Pascal et al., 2019, p. 7)

Being active and engaging in other areas of learning generates further opportunities for physical activity and is the beginning of children developing their CL, which then supports relationship building, understanding of feelings and learning about themselves, where they fit within the wider world and community and their physical wellbeing.

COMMUNICATION AND LANGUAGE

In the first version of the EYFS in 2008, communication, language and literacy were combined as a single area of learning; however, from 2011 onwards literacy became a separate early learning objective. While they are separated, it is important to emphasise that they are closely related components of complex learning and development processes. As you progress through the chapters in this book you will see the interconnected nature of the areas of learning and be able to make links across them. This is particularly noticeable for CL. In the statutory EYFS it is the first area of learning outlined because there is widespread recognition that the development of CL is central to the whole process of learning.

We use language (both verbally and non-verbally) as the primary means by which we convey meaning – such as emotions, thoughts, ideas – and communicate with others. When we learn to use words to describe objects, situations, or concepts, it becomes symbolic. Symbols (words) in language are composed of small sounds. Phonemes are the sounds that we combine to form words (Palaiologou, 2021).

Phonology (phonemes): The combination of sounds that form a word.

Semantics: A set of skills used to make sure that all parties involved in communication understand the meaning of the symbols we use.

Syntax: After mastering the understanding of words, we are able to start putting them together into sentences that follow a set of rules.

Pragmatics: When we use language to communicate, we use gestures, smiles, eye contact and intonations in our voice in addition to words and sentences.

The development of language is impacted by the environment. Language development is not a standalone concept; the environment plays a vital part in supporting language development. When children are born, they mainly use crying as a way to communicate their needs. However, babies are starting to understand and are able to respond to different types of sounds, not only in their own language but other languages too (Gerken, 1994). Developing children's receptive and spoken language is crucial.

COMMUNICATION AND LANGUAGE IN PRACTICE

Table 3.1 Activities within practice to enhance communication and language

Activities	Examples in practice
Interactions	From an early age, children are able to interact with others, beginning to lay the foundation for the development of language and cognitive skills. To ensure a child's development, it is necessary to create interactions throughout the day and provide a language-rich environment.
Conversations	It is important to have conversations together. Children learn by example: when adults comment on what they are interested in or doing, children then repeat what they say using new vocabulary. By engaging children in a conversation, practitioners will effectively build children's language skills.
Reading	It is important to read frequently to children in order to develop their vocabulary and listening skills. Make sure they are actively engaged in stories, nonfiction, rhymes and poems. In addition, provide them with numerous opportunities to practise and embed new words in a variety of contexts, such as writing and speaking. This will provide children with the opportunity to thrive and learn new words while enjoying the experience.

PHYSICAL DEVELOPMENT

Babies and young children have an innate desire to play. Within Western societies it is generally accepted that young children learn through play. This is mirrored in the United Nations Convention on the Right of the Child (UNCRC) (UNICEF, 1989) and states that play is a fundamental right for children; this view is echoed within the fibres of the EYFS and across many societies today.

Movement and other physical attributes to development do not happen in isolation; PSED, movement and coordination, CL, creativity and developing curiosity are all intertwined, and bringing them together lays the foundations for all learning. It is claimed that children think with their bodies and their minds (Mountain, 2017). Therefore, physical and active play is not only a vehicle for physical development and exercise, but it also promotes and enhances many different areas of development. For babies, The World Health Organization (WHO, 2019) recommends that babies who are not yet mobile should spend 30 minutes a day in prone position (tummy time), spread throughout the day while awake.

PHYSICAL DEVELOPMENT IN PRACTICE

Young children's level of physical activities vary and are affected by their environments. As argued by Rodriguez Leon (2024, p. 94):

> Babies and young children have an innate desire to play. In contemporary Western cultures, it is generally accepted that young children learn through play.

Most young children will be active, but it is important to reflect on how we arrange the environment, especially indoors, and limit the movement of children. Physical activities need to be thought of and integrated into daily practices, and these ideas can be incorporated into everyday opportunities.

Table 3.2 Activities to support physical development

Activities	Examples in practice
Different spaces for movement	To create such spaces indoors, furniture can be moved to the sides of the room to allow for unimpeded movement or a hallway can be turned into a play area. Children have the opportunity to gain a different perspective on their own body in space through big open spaces in the outdoor environment. Furthermore, young children should be exposed to a variety of surfaces, such as grass, sand, pebbles, woodchips, carpets, concrete and playground 'soft surfaces'. It has been shown that different terrains, with uneven surfaces or gradients, provide unique sensory feedback that contributes to developing balance, self-awareness and control (White, 2015).
Floor time	It is beneficial for children to spend time on the floor, especially if they are accompanied by their caregiver. By lifting their legs and grasping their feet, babies develop proprioception and strengthen their abdominal muscles while lying on their backs. The muscles in the back, neck and arms are strengthened when people spend time in 'prone position', i.e. lying on their stomachs. In order for babies to focus their vision and grasp objects, it is helpful to place a few toys nearby.

(Continued)

Table 3.2 (Continued)

Activities	Examples in practice
Movement, dance and music	It is important to develop fine and gross motor control with nursery rhymes and songs that include action, such as 'The wheels on the bus', 'Wind the bobbin up'. These activities also promote language and communication development, as well as social and emotional wellbeing.
Pushing, pulling, lifting	In order to provide opportunities for pushing, pulling and lifting, a variety of objects (wooden blocks, pebbles, ropes for throwing over trees and climbing apparatus, or old tyres) should be available for the children. Besides being physically challenging, this type of play also develops children's understanding of concepts such as size, weight, shape, volume and capacity, as well as writing skills.
Mark-making	In addition to incorporating up and down movements, side-to-side movements and circular movements, vertical surfaces, such as painting easels or blackboards, also encourage large whole-arm movements. Children can paint outside walls or the playground with large paint brushes or rollers if the weather is warm. It is also enjoyable to use spray bottles with water to develop the muscles in the hands and wrists.

PERSONAL, SOCIAL AND EMOTIONAL DEVELOPMENT

For children to lead healthy and happy lives, they need to develop their personal, social and emotional skills (PSED). It is an essential component of their cognitive development. A variety of important attachments are created as a result of their personal development. Children's attachments and relationships can have a significant impact on their social development. Relationships with adults that are warm, supportive and strong enable children to develop an understanding of their own feelings and those of others. Bradbury and Grimmer (2024) argue that love and nurture needs to be at the foreground of Early Years practice, and this is why PSED is so important.

The Early Years environment should be a place where children can be supported to manage their emotions, develop a sense of belonging and a sense of self, and be able to have confidence in developing their own abilities. The early years in a child's life are a valuable time for PSED. To be as effective as possible, this development must take place in an environment which is safe, secure, affectionate and enables children, but also an environment which promotes feelings and social skills (for more information on this, see Chapter 5, this volume).

SPECIFIC AREAS

In contrast to the prime areas described in the EYFS, the specific areas are not time-sensitive – that is, the brain and body undergo significant developmental changes in the prime areas in the first five years of life, in particular, and if these are secured children are better placed to achieve well in their learning. The specific areas are important and should be used to provide a broad curriculum through which children can develop their early skills. Because of our current assessment system in England, only two of the four specific areas are included in the *good level of development*, the measure which the DfE use to assess whether children are 'ready' for Year 1. It is our belief that this is a missed opportunity and can lead to the two areas which are not included, *expressive arts and design* and *understanding the world*, being sidelined and viewed as less important. We know that all learning is interconnected and that these areas of learning will provide a useful means of supporting children to make sense of the world around them and their role within it, which is vital for developing children's personal, social and emotional skills. As part of the EYFS *Development Matters* (DfE, 2021) framework, the first three prime areas are explored, followed by the four specific areas. Our belief is much more aligned to having them all as ELGs as we would argue that they are all interlinked and add much value to the child and/or practices when developed more holistically.

It is important to note that both the prime and specific areas of learning are guided by the overarching principles that guide practice in early childhood settings. In accordance with the Statutory Framework for the EYFS, there are four guiding principles:

- every child is a *unique child*, who is constantly learning and can be resilient, capable, confident and self-assured;
- children learn to be strong and independent through *positive relationships*;
- children learn and develop well in *enabling environments with teaching and support from adults*, who respond to their individual interests and needs and help them to build their learning over time. Children benefit from a strong partnership between practitioners and parents and/or carers;
- importance of *learning and development*. Children develop and learn at different rates.

The four specific areas in EYFS are:

1. literacy
2. mathematics
3. understanding the world
4. expressive arts and design.

LITERACY

According to the EYFS, communication and language are two of the most important areas of learning. Although literacy (reading and writing) is a specific area of development, it is understood that these are regarded as being central to a child's development in order to support specific aspects of development. Often, emergent literacy refers to a child's early experiences with reading and writing. Children's understanding of the functions and purposes of reading and writing develops in many ways according to emergent approaches. As young children are not able to read and write at the time of birth, the term 'emergent' acknowledges the need for them to develop.

In research such as socio-cultural theory, it has been found that children learn literacy through active engagement with both their social and cultural environments (Barrat-Pugh and Rohl, 2020). By interacting with a more competent member of society, Vygotsky (1978) argued that cultural knowledge is transmitted to an individual, who is then able to internalise and incorporate the new ideas and concepts. Due to this, it is reasonable to assume that children will begin to naturally infer the semiotic and functional nature of written language while living and participating in an environment that offers written language to print for a variety of reasons.

CASE STUDY 3.1

LITERACY SKILLS

An Early Years teacher is developing a role play area on the theme of shops. The teacher started to think about what they could incorporate into the area to support literacy skills. They decided to ask the children what shops they go to and painted a backdrop of items which the children buy from the shops – including till roll paper and pens; the children were given opportunities to write shopping lists to go shopping in the supermarket.

Following the children's interests, many writing opportunities emerged:

- children started to draw their own produce and stick it on the wall; with the support of an adult they modelled the spelling of the items;
- they made lists of items to buy in the shops;
- they used numbers to attempt adding up pennies and put the prices onto the items;
- they wrote letters to each other; one of the children had an elderly relative and explained that his mum goes to the relative's home and they give her a letter;
- some children wrote down a set of instructions on where to go if the items were not in the supermarket;
- some children started to draw and paint other supermarkets and the role play area extended out into the classroom.

Writing at the beginning

It takes children a considerable amount of time to learn to write. The development of writing is based on two main factors: first, a development of writing skills (fine motor skills such as hand–eye coordination and the ability to hold and manipulate a writing instrument); second, developing compositional skills (the ability to comprehend and apply organisational elements such as spelling and grammar).

Characteristics of early writing

1. *Making marks*. Children may describe the marks they make on paper when asked about them. Even if they do not appear to be drawings at all, they may explain that they are words.
2. *Symbols*. When they begin to describe the symbols and things they see as writing, they may start to see them as an emergence of letters.
3. *Incorporation*. In the course of their play, children will begin to write messages and lists. In spite of the fact that the formation of letters may not be legible, they are forming.
4. *Name recognition*. Eventually, children will be able to recognise their own names in print and begin to write them, perhaps by copying first and then writing independently. Though their efforts may not closely resemble their names, the child is able to recognise them and understand what they mean.
5. *Writing*. What children write will be expected to be readable by adults and others.

MATHEMATICS

In the foundation curriculum, mathematics focuses on two main areas: *number* and *numerical patterns*.

- In *number*, children are taught counting, addition and subtraction, along with number work and number problems.
- The purpose of *numerical patterns* is to recognise and represent patterns as they count, compare numbers and identify differences between them.

In order for children to excel in mathematics, they must develop a strong grounding in numbers. To achieve this goal, children should be able to confidently count up to ten and understand the relationships between those numbers, as well as the patterns within those numbers. The development of a secure foundation of knowledge and vocabulary that will serve as the basis for mastery of mathematics will be achieved if children receive frequent and varied opportunities to build and apply this understanding – such as manipulatives, including small pebbles and tens frames for organising counting.

In previous iterations of the EYFS, *shape, space and measure* has been an area of learning with a specific goal. Controversially, this goal was removed in the 2020 curriculum.

Some people now believe that it is not as important for young children's learning because it is no longer a goal. However, it is mentioned in the educational programme and remains a vital element of our statutory curriculum. It is important the curriculum includes many opportunities for children to develop their spatial awareness, reasoning skills and the concept of shapes across all areas of mathematics. It is important that we foster of a love of mathematics from an early age and ask the children to 'have a go'. Adults need to nurture children's opportunities to make mistakes, make connections and learn through an adoption of play-based learning, both in the form of child- and adult-led opportunities.

UNDERSTANDING THE WORLD

There are three key areas covered in *understanding the world*:

- developing an understanding of people, cultures and communities – children are introduced to different cultures and religious beliefs, as well as the contributions made by each individual to society;
- children are introduced to the natural world in order to gain a greater understanding of the seasons and other living organisms;
- it is essential that children begin to understand and articulate differences between the past and present as they examine prior and contemporary events.

This is an area of learning which changed significantly when the EYFS was reformed in 2020. It is clear to see the links to the Key Stage 1 areas of History, Geography and Science, but it is important to remember that the development of this area is also linked to children's sense of self and PSED. Through developing their understanding of the wider world beyond themselves and their immediate family, children will make sense of the world around them and their place within it.

Goals can drive some of the curriculum content, as was fed back to the DfE by 24 schools involved in a pilot scheme. It is important to remember that, even though we have the goals in mind, the curriculum should be shaped by the educational programmes and the needs, interests and starting points of the children.

EXPRESSIVE ARTS AND DESIGN

From the perspective of the other areas of development, this may appear to be the final area of learning. As such it can sometimes be the 'poorer relation' of the specific areas. It should, however, be noted that this area of learning is vital for fostering the child's imagination and enabling them to express themselves in a variety of ways by taking advantage of the skills acquired in other prime and specific domains of their development. Young children will often make sense of the world around them using role play, narrative and other types of creative expression such as mark making, dance and music.

This area of learning explores:

- *making and presenting art using materials*: children are encouraged to experiment with different methods of creating and presenting art. As part of this process, we will examine various media, such as drawings or sculptures, and different materials, such as colouring, painting, or building;
- *the ability to think creatively and express themselves*: children's ability to come up with their own ideas, pictures, and ways of expressing themselves.

Through *expressive arts and design*, children are given the freedom to express themselves using the media and outlets they are most comfortable with, preparing them for a successful future as confident, self-assured individuals. Children's imagination and creativity are supported by their artistic and cultural awareness. A variety of media and materials can be explored and played with by children who are regularly exposed to the arts. Increasing children's vocabulary, understanding, self-expression and ability to communicate through the arts depends on the quality and variety of what they see, hear and participate in. Interpretation and appreciation of what they hear, respond to and observe depends on the frequency, repetition and depth of their experiences.

REFLECTION 3.1

- Does your approach to the curriculum reflect the importance of the prime areas? Do they underpin all other areas of learning?
- How much time do children get to revise and revisit their prior learning?
- How much time are children able to spend in the continuous provision refining their skills and knowledge?

Does your timetable and your curriculum reflect your children's needs and your key priorities?

KEY POINTS OF THE CHAPTER

The educational programmes provide us with a broad overview of the concepts, knowledge and skills children should develop during their time in the Foundation Stage. It is up to practitioners to decide how children develop these and what they need to learn, based on the specific needs of their individual children. When designing a curriculum, it can be helpful to have an overview of the key knowledge, skills and dispositions we want to develop with our children, but it is also vital to ensure we leave room to follow children's interests, to develop the voice of the child and meet their unique needs. It is important to ensure that we do not put so much content into our curriculum that we miss opportunities for children to revisit learning, to practise, to explore, to refine their skills and to go deeper with their learning by using the skills and knowledge we have taught them across a range of different areas. This is why it is important to think carefully about the structure of our day: how much time is spent in adult-directed activity; how much is spent in child-initiated learning; or in adult-initiated learning in the continuous provision. There are no rules about how long should be spent on each area of learning or on the way these areas should be taught. There are lots of pedagogical decisions to be made and many will be based on the unique cohort of children. It is important to reflect on your priorities based on your children and build your plans accordingly.

REFERENCES

Barrat-Pugh, C. and Rohl, M. (2020) *Literacy Learning in the Early Years*. London: Routledge.

Bradbury, A. and Grimmer, T. (2024) *Love and Nurture in the Early Years*. London: Learning Matters.

Department for Education (DfE) (2021) *Development Matters: Non-Statutory Curriculum Guidance for the Early Years Foundation Stage*. Available at: https://assets.publishing.service.gov.uk/media/64e6002a20ae890014f26cbc/DfE_Development_Matters_Report_Sep2023.pdf [Accessed 1 January 2024].

DfE (2023) *Early Years Foundation Stage Profile: 2024 Handbook*. Available at: https://assets.publishing.service.gov.uk/media/65253bc12548ca000dddf050/EYFSP_2024_handbook.pdf [Accessed 28 May 2024].

Early Years Coalition (2021) *Birth to 5 Matters Non-statutory Guidance to the Early Years Foundation Stage*. Available at: https://birthto5matters.org.uk/wp-content/uploads/2021/03/Birthto5Matters-download.pdf [Accessed 1 January 2024].

Gerken, L. (1994) Young children's representation of prosodic phonology: Evidence from English-speakers' weak syllable productions. *Journal of Memory and Language*, 33(1), 19–38.

Grimmer, T. (2021) *Developing a Loving Pedagogy in the Early Years: How Love Fits with Professional Practice*. London: Routledge.

Mountain, J. (2017) *Outdoors and Active*. London.: Early Education.

Palaiologou, I. (2021) *The Early Years Foundation Stage: Theory and Practice*. London: Sage.

Pascal, C., Bertram, T. and Rouse, L. (2019) *Getting it Right in the Early Years Foundation Stage: A Review of the Evidence*. Early Education. Available at: https://early-education.org.uk/wp-content/uploads/2021/12/Getting-it-right-in-the-EYFS-Literature-Review.pdf [Accessed 1 January 2024].

Rodriguez Leon, L. (2024) Play and physical development in early childhood. In J. Musgrave, J. Dorrian, J. Josephidou, B. Langdown and L. Rodriguez Leon, *Promoting Physical Development and Activity in Early Childhood: Practical Ideas for Early Years Settings* (Chapter 5). London: Routledge.

Tickell, C. (2011) *The Early Years: Foundations for Life, Health and Learning. An Independent Report on the Early Years Foundation Stage to Her Majesty's Government*. Available at: https://assets.publishing.service.gov.uk/media/5a7ac0ec40f0b66a2fc02915/DFE-00177-2011.pdf [Accessed 1 January 2024].

UNICEF (1989) United Nations Convention on the Rights of the Child. Available at: www.unicef.org.uk/wp-content/uploads/2016/08/unicef-convention-rights-child-uncrc.pdf [Accessed 28 May 2024].

Vygotsky L.S. (1978) *Mind in Society: The Development of Higher Psychological Processes*. Cambridge, MA: Harvard University Press.

White, J. (2015) *Every Child a Mover: A Practical Guide to Providing Your Children with the Physical Opportunities They Need*. London: British Association for Early Childhood Education.

World Health Organization (WHO) (2019) *Guidelines on Physical Activity. Sedentary Behaviour and Sleep for Children under 5 Years of Age. Geneva*. Available at: https://apps.who.int/iris/handle/10665/311664 [Accessed 1 December 2023].

4

COMMUNICATION AND LANGUAGE

> *The development of children's spoken language underpins all seven areas of learning.*
>
> DfE, 2023

INTRODUCTION

The importance of communication and language skills in the Early Years has been widely recognised and undisputed for decades. Bruner (1983) points out that adult–child conversation begins before the child has any language of their own, as babies respond sensitively to their caregiver's facial expressions and the pair take turns in 'conversation' through eye contact, gesture and utterances.

Extensive research studies have identified that children's early language skills are a strong and significant indicator of their future outcomes and development. Dockrell et al. (2010), commissioned by the DfE, emphasise how responsive early interactions lay the foundations for later literacy. In 2011, Snowling and Hulme's review revealed that there was considerable evidence to show that language skills are amongst the best predictors of educational success. Findings from a population-based longitudinal study of parents and children in the UK indicate that language development at the age of two years predicts children's performance on entering primary school (Roulstone et al., 2011).

They also showed that children who enter school with poorly developed speech and language are at high risk of literacy difficulties and educational underachievement is common in such children. More recently, DfE statistics (2022) have shown that there is an increasing number of children entering our settings with speech, language and communication delays; this is likely to impact on their overall attainment in the long term.

- In 2022, 25.1 per cent of the 1.49 million children with identified SEND in England have speech, language and communication needs (SLCN).
- SLCN is the most commonly identified SEND for children in receipt of SEN support in England at the moment.
- 59 per cent of four-year-olds on SEN support have SLCN.
- In areas of poverty, over 50 per cent of children are starting school with delayed communication skills.
- Their speech may be unclear, vocabulary is smaller, sentences are shorter and they are able to understand only simple instructions. Many of these children can catch up with the right support.
- 50–90 per cent of children with persistent speech, language and communication difficulties go on to have reading difficulties.
- Two-thirds of seven- to 14-year-olds with serious behaviour problems have language impairment.
- At least 60 per cent of young people in young offender institutions have communication difficulties.
- Those with a history of early language impairment are at higher risk of mental health problems – for example, 2.7 times more likely of having a social phobia by age 19.

This is quite a worrying picture; however, according to the same report:

> When language difficulties are resolved by the age of 5 and a half, children are more likely to go on to develop good reading and spelling skills. This good performance continues throughout their school careers and they pass as many exams on leaving school as children without a history of speech, language and communication difficulties.
>
> (DfE, 2022)

It is no surprise then that the most recent iteration of the EYFS (DfE, 2023) places a huge emphasis on the importance of children's language, not just within the communication educational programme quoted above, but within most areas of the curriculum.

In the PSED programme, 'Strong, warm and supportive relationships with adults enable children to learn how to understand their own feelings and those of others … Through *supported interaction* with other children they learn how to make good friendships, co-operate and resolve conflicts peaceably' (DfE, 2023).

In literacy, 'Language comprehension (necessary for both reading and writing) starts from birth. It only develops when adults talk with children about the world around them and the books (stories and non-fiction) they read with them, and enjoy rhymes, poems and songs together' (DfE, 2023, p. 7).

In understanding the world, 'listening to a broad selection of stories, non-fiction, rhymes and poems will foster their understanding of our culturally, socially, technologically and ecologically diverse world' (DfE, 2023, p. 7).

In maths, 'It is important that children develop positive attitudes and interests, "have a go", talk to adults and peers about what they notice and not be afraid to make mistakes' (DfE, 2023, p. 7). Soto-Calvo et al. (2015) identify oral language skills as impacting on the development of counting and calculations. And in expressive arts and design, 'The quality and variety of what children see, hear and participate in is crucial for developing their understanding, self-expression, vocabulary and ability to communicate through the arts' (DfE, 2023, p. 7).

Many of the ELGs require children to be adept communicators and would be difficult for children to achieve without good expression and understanding. Thus, language and communication are central to all areas of learning, although it is interesting to note that many of the ELGs require excellent understanding rather than just the spoken language mentioned in the DfE educational programme. It is important to realise that children's spoken language is often just the tip of a very large iceberg. What they articulate demonstrates only one area of their language and communication development.

HOW LANGUAGE DEVELOPS

It would be impossible in a single chapter to go into the depth required to cover all aspects of early language development. However, research has shown us that from before birth babies are able to tune into their mother's voices in the womb (Karmiloff and Karmiloff-Smith, 2002) and from birth babies communicate their needs through expressions such as crying, cooing, gazing, etc. These 'serve and return' interactions are known to help build brain architecture. Neuro-imaging research has given us greater insight into the impact of early language experiences on young children's brains and their development:

> children who experienced more conversational turns exhibited greater activation in left inferior frontal regions (Broca's area) during language processing, which explained nearly half the relationship between children's language exposure and verbal abilities.
>
> (Romeo et al., 2018)

From birth, babies are communicating with their caregivers, using their bodies, movement, facial expressions and cries to communicate their needs. One of the predecessor documents to the EYFS, *Birth to Three Matters* (Abbott and Langston, 2005), acknowledged and celebrated the concept of young children as confident communicators. We also know that young children can often follow an instruction before they are able to verbalise their thoughts. As previously stated (see Chapter 3), the Tickell review identified language and communication as a prime area because of the time-sensitive nature of language development: 'Communication and language skills are at their most sensitive to development between birth and 7 years of age and are "experience expectant"' (Tickell, 2011, Annex 8, 98).

As children grow and develop, they learn to tune into and locate a range of sounds, and to distinguish between them. Young babies will often quieten to the sound of speech and look intently at the person who is talking and, as children grow and develop, they may turn to face sounds they enjoy and will enjoy playing games such as peek-a-boo and action rhymes. Here, children are learning about the early interplay between themselves and others, that communication is a social activity and that their actions can impact on others. Initially, young babies are tuning into what is known as 'Motherese' (Gleitman et al., 1984), where the adult involved uses higher pitched intonation and speaks at a slower pace to encourage the child to tune in. Motherese consists of short, grammatically simple sentences, often accompanied by gestures. Young children will often respond to simple instructions such as 'throw ball' before they are able to articulate them.

As children develop awareness that their sounds generate a response from adults and begin to tune into words which are meaningful to them, they will begin to make noises and eventually simple words to communicate their needs. Babbling becomes increasingly word-like and in time babies use phrases which are regularly repeated, 'bye bye' or 'no' or 'all gone'. Eventually, these phrases become more complex, putting two or three words together, following simple instructions, showing they understand the language they're being exposed to. On average, a two-year-old will have between 250 and 300 words, increasing to around 1,000 by age three. Three-year-olds are usually able to put phrases of three to four words together and by the age of four children should be using around 1,500 words, be able to follow simple three-part instructions (e.g., point to the door, the window and the floor) and understand more complex sentences. Many will understand concepts such as behind, above, under, over and may understand and ask what, where, when and how questions. Some children will need support with this and we need to consider how we design our curriculum to ensure that the development of language is central to children's learning.

WHAT DOES THIS MEAN FOR OUR CURRICULUM?

Bingham and Whitebread (2018) identified that in order to develop self-regulation and executive function, which are vital to higher-order thinking skills such as problem-solving, reasoning and planning, children need good language and communications skills.

Ideally, our communication educational programme should focus on more than just the spoken word and incorporate important skills such as understanding, listening and attention.

However, there is much that is of merit in the DfE educational programme and it is pleasing that communication has been given prominence as the first ELG. Without communication, all other areas are going to be challenging to achieve. There is extensive research evidence to back up the importance of a language-rich curriculum (Dockrell et al., 2010; Pascal et al., 2017; Pascal et al., 2019; Payler et al., 2017; Snowling and Hulme, 2011). It is clear that we need to place language at the heart of our curriculum.

It's impossible to talk about communication and language and not mention the huge focus on vocabulary in recent years and the much-cited 'word gap' research (Hart and Risley, 1995) which underpins some of the current thinking in the Ofsted framework. This study has been critiqued by researchers such as Ian Cushing (2022), Sperry et al. (2019) and Gilkerson et al. (2017) due to the methods, potential racial bias and 'failed replications'; however, there have been counter critiques of the further research. Again, there is not enough space within this chapter to explore the issues fully, but wider reading of the cited research is highly likely to be of interest to those working with young children. What we do know is that talking to and with children really matters; however, it is widely accepted that vocabulary alone is not enough.

Michael Jones, in his book *Talking and Learning with Young Children* (2016), identifies four key elements a good talker needs: some words (vocabulary); somewhere to talk; someone to talk to; something to talk about.

We need to consider these important elements in our current provision:

> When I'm working with staff, I get them to consider what happens in their settings right now, and we use a simple grid to conduct some appreciative inquiry (see Figure 4.1).
>
> (Cooperrider, 1986)

By focusing on what is already happening and a strength in the setting, it is possible to identify how we can develop further.

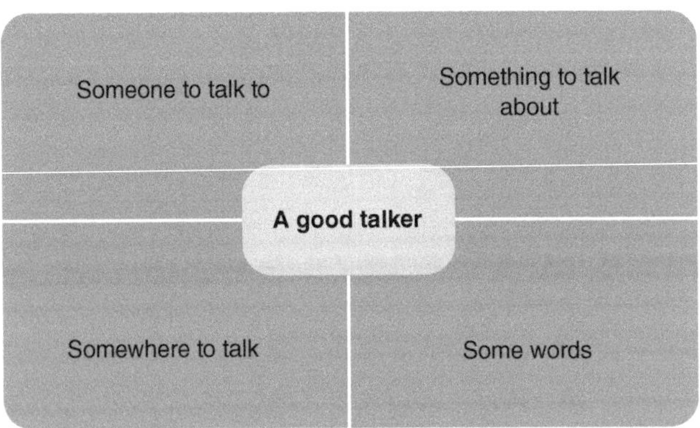

Figure 4.1 Appreciative inquiry grid for talk in the learning environment, designed by Swailes, inspired by the work of Michael Jones and David Cooperrider

Using the simple grid model shown in Figure 4.1, I ask staff to think and reflect over the course of a typical week. Where do they hear children talking a lot? What are the children really excited to talk about? Who are they talking to (this might be an adult in the setting or other children)? What words are they using? How were they introduced to these words?

It's then helpful for everyone to share their findings and discuss what they notice. Sharing the findings from the whole team often reveals that different staff have different perceptions based on their roles within the team and this can be useful to spark discussions.

Identifying strengths is good for team morale but it also helps us to think about why things are good. Why are children particularly chatty in the block play area? What is it about the recent topic about families that's made them so excited to talk to each other? Once you've unpicked what it is about a certain aspect you've identified as a strength, you can start to think about how you might replicate this in other areas.

MORE THAN JUST WORDS

Words and vocabulary are important, but words alone are not enough to support children's language development. Kathy Hirsh-Pasek et al. (2015) argue that the richness, variety and depth of language interactions truly shape children's linguistic abilities and that meaningful conversations and engaging language experiences are vital for developing young children's early communication skills. I am always a little troubled when I see lists of abstract words that children are going to learn in the name of developing their communication skills, when they seem unrelated to things children are naturally interested in and more related to the content children will need to learn in Key Stages 1 and 2. While it's important to expose children to lots of language and vocabulary, it is important that we start with what is meaningful to them as very young children. I've seen curricula which introduce vocabulary related to artistic impressionism to three-year-olds, with seemingly no thought for the fact that they probably have between 1,500 and 2,000 words, all of which are likely to relate to things which are deeply meaningful to them. This is often promoted as being ambitious, but it will likely be far too abstract a concept for the children to fully understand.

The work of Beck, McKeown and Kucan (Beck et al., 2013) can be really useful when working with older children (their initial studies were with children aged five to six and six to seven, the equivalent to Year 1 and Year 2 children in the UK), but dividing vocabulary into tiers for two-year-olds is probably not helpful.

HOW CAN WE PLAN FOR EFFECTIVE COMMUNICATION?

There are lots of different types of talk that happen in the classroom. Some is teacher talk, some is adult-led communication in the continuous provision, some will be child-initiated discussions, led by children's interest. Some talk we can plan for – for example, if we know we will be teaching a specific topic there may be some key vocabulary that we want to make sure the children know; this is where the work of Beck, McKeown and Kucan can be helpful. We can consider what the children may already know, and then think about key vocabulary that is essential for them to understand the concept we're teaching. For example, if we are introducing young children to the concept of weight, we might choose some tier 2 (academic) vocabulary related to this subject such as *heavier, lighter, heavy, light, balance*. However, when working with young children it's unlikely that we'd progress on to low-frequency concept-specific tier 3 words such as grams, kilograms and mass.

Of course, language development doesn't just happen in the large and small group work we plan with the children. Using our appreciative inquiry tools to identify the spaces where children like to speak, we can try to understand what it is about the area that might promote such lively discussions. By spending time in an area of provision and considering what learning might happen there and the sort of vocabulary we *might* naturally use it is possible to plan for effective interactions and communication in the continuous provision.

We can't always plan exactly how the conversations will go, but if we're working in an area, we can probably plan for some of the language and vocabulary that might occur. The work of Julie Fisher on sustaining effective interactions (2016) provides a really useful lens when considering the kind of interactions that *might* happen in an area of provision.

LET'S USE THE WATER AREA AS AN EXAMPLE

Commenting

- 'The water is cold', 'I'm putting my hands in the water', 'I'm filling the jug', 'I'm pouring into the bucket.'
- Naming simple objects, such as *boat, jug, bucket, funnel*. These are particularly helpful strategies for children who are new to English or in the early stages of developing verbal language.
- Introducing specific vocabulary; depending on children's understanding vocabulary such as *pour, fill, empty, full, half full, cold, warm, float* and *sink* might be introduced into the water.

Imagining

Some children might use the water to recreate a narrative – for example, using sea creatures to tell a story. This would enable the introduction of storying language such as 'Let's pretend we can see a magic world at the bottom', 'What might it feel like to be under the water?' 'What might happen when we get to the bottom?'

Pondering

Pondering is a great way to ask children questions without them feeling under pressure. It also demonstrates and models thinking out loud to children, which is vital for developing their executive function skills. The adult is demonstrating that they might not have all the answers and the child has agency in the discussion.

'I wonder what might happen if I keep pouring?' when filling up the buckets.

'I wonder whether this one holds more water than this one?'

Connecting

Connecting to prior learning is also powerful and helps children to understand that their learning is linked, 'Do you remember when we poured the water into this container?', 'Can you fill that by yourself today? You had a good try yesterday.' This helps children bring their previous successes to mind and is excellent for their esteem and their understanding of their own learning.

Posing problems

This allows children to use their prior knowledge to try to resolve new problems.

'I wonder if there's a way to make sure everyone has a turn with the water wheel?'

'How might we make sure we don't slip on the wet floor?'

Explaining

'The jug is heavy when it's full, you might need both hands to lift it.'

'When the water goes on the floor it makes things slippy.'

Thinking out loud

This is a powerful way to promote children's own thinking and shows children that adults don't always know the answers; they have to try new things and be willing to have a go. It is an ideal way to model the characteristics of effective learning. 'I think I'll try to fill this bucket with this jug.' 'I remember I used this one yesterday.'

OTHER IDEAS

You might also consider some of the other conversations that might occur based on your children's current understanding and interests, the things you've already taught them and the resources you've chosen. Of course, it's impossible to prepare for every interaction, that's the beauty of working with young children, but by thinking carefully about possibilities, staff can develop their confidence to have meaningful interactions with the children linked to their interests and needs, rather than trying to shoehorn vocabulary and questions into conversations.

Finally, Fisher (2016) reminds us that there are times when staying quiet is the best option.

STAYING QUIET

It is important to remember that silence is powerful. Children need time to process and reflect on their learning. Over time staff become more confident to do this, as they get to know the children well.

By thinking about each area of provision in this way we can develop staff confidence in interacting with the children and they can build meaningful relationships with the children secure in the knowledge that they are supporting sustained shared thinking in an appropriate way.

TIME TO COMMUNICATE

Hopefully, this chapter has reinforced the importance of language and communication in developing young children's learning. If we look at the statutory educational programmes and ELGs alongside the characteristics of effective learning (Early Years Coalition, 2021, pp. 52–54) we can see that it is almost impossible to achieve success in the EYFS without good communication and language. Moreover, research is clear that language and communication is critical for lifelong learning and success. In their 2016 study, *The State of Speaking in Our Schools*, Millard and Menzies asked teachers about oracy: 68 per cent agreed that it is very important, but 31 per cent said they didn't have time to develop it. Given the DfE's own statistics (2022) around the long-term impact of poor communication and language, it seems impossible to understand that almost a third of teachers feel they don't have time to incorporate oracy into every day. However, if we consider why this might be the case, an additional challenge faced by teachers and schools wanting to develop and extend oracy is that there is 'nothing to show for it'. Interviewees felt this was a response to 'high stakes' accountability, wherein teachers feel under pressure to ensure children produce lots of writing (Millard and Menzies, 2016).

All too often the value of talk is discussed, but the timetables and plans staff are asked to follow do not match the rhetoric. There is no point focusing on the interactions, vocabulary, language and communication we might use with children and spending time developing superb provision to support this, if everything in the setting focuses on adult-led learning and the timetable is crammed with direct instruction. We know that promoting higher-order literacy skills before children have a secure development in oral language will lead to problems for these children (Dockrell et al., 2010; Payler et al, 2017; Pascal et al., 2017), yet all too often, particularly in the later stages of the EYFS, talk is seen as a means to an end, rather than as an end in itself. It is useful to look at timetables and consider whether enough time is spent supporting children's opportunities to talk.

REFLECTION 4.1

Are there opportunities for children to spend time in continuous provision every day?

Do adults value children's talk or are they under pressure to produce outcomes in other areas? Is talk valued in its own right?

Who does the most talking?

In 'serve and return' conversations, who serves the most?

KEY POINTS OF THE CHAPTER

Language and communication underpin all other areas of learning.

Spoken language is merely the tip of the iceberg; young children's language development is complex, with their understanding of receptive language, grammar, structure, cultural nuance, social and contextual meaning developing alongside their articulation.

Children benefit from high-quality interactions with adults who are interested in them, 'sustained shared thinking occurs most successfully in a 1:1 or 1:2 situation' (Siraj-Blatchford et al., 2002). This does not need to be a prolonged interaction, the practitioner's contribution can be brief or extended; it is the quality that matters.

Silence is important – children need time and space to absorb and reflect; this is particularly important for children who are new to learning English who often go through a phase of 'intent participation' (Tabors, 1997) where they observe but don't always contribute.

REFERENCES

Abbott, L. and Langston, A. (2005) *Birth to Three Matters: Supporting the Framework of Effective Practice*. London: Open University Press.

Beck, I.L., McKeown, M.G. and Kucan, L. (2013) *Bringing Words to Life: Robust Vocabulary Instruction*. New York: Guilford Press.

Bingham, S. and Whitebread, D. (2018) School readiness in Europe: Issues and evidence. In J.L. Roopnarine, J.E. Johnson, S.F. Quinn and M.M. Patte, *International Handbook of Early Childhood Education* (pp. 363–391). London: Routledge.

Bruner, J. (1983) *Child's Talk: Learning to Use Language*. New York: Norton.

Cooperrider, D.L. (1986) Appreciative inquiry: Toward a methodology for understanding and enhancing organizational innovation. Unpublished doctoral dissertation. Case Western Reserve University, Cleveland, Ohio.

Cooperrider, D. (2023) *Appreciative Inquiry at Champlain College*. Available at: https://appreciativeinquiry.champlain.edu/people/cooperrider-ph-d-david-l-1139/ [Accessed 6 April 2024].

Cushing, I. (2022) Word rich or word poor? Deficit discourses, raciolinguistic ideologies and the resurgence of the 'word gap' in England's education policy. *Critical Inquiry in Language Studies*, 20(4), 305–331.

Department for Education (DfE) (2022) *Special Educational Needs in England, Academic Year 2021/22*. Available at: https://explore-education-statistics.service.gov.uk/find-statistics/special-educational-needs-in-england/2021-22 [Accessed 12 April 2024].

DfE (2023) *Early Years Foundation Stage Statutory Framework*. Available at: www.gov.uk/government/publications/early-years-foundation-stage-framework--2 [Accessed 28 May 2024].

Dockrell, J.E., Stuart, M. and King, D. (2010) Supporting early oral language skills for English language learners in inner city preschool provision. *British Journal of Educational Psychology*, 80(4), 497–515.

Early Years Coalition (2021) *Birth to 5 Matters Non-statutory Guidance to the Early Years Foundation Stage*. Available at: https://birthto5matters.org.uk/wp-content/uploads/2021/03/Birthto5Matters-download.pdf [Accessed 1 January 2024].

Fisher, J. (2016) *Interacting or Interfering? Improving Interactions in the Early Years*. Berkshire: McGraw-Hill Education.

Gilkerson, J., Richards, J.A., Warren, S.F., Montgomery, J.K., Greenwood, C.R., Kimbrough-Oller, D., Hansen, J.H.L. and Paul, T.D. (2017) Mapping the early language environment using all-day recordings and automated analysis. *American Journal of Speech-Language Pathology*, 26(2), 248–265.

Gleitman, L.R., Newport, E.L. and Gleitman, H. (1984) The current status of the Motherese hypothesis. *Journal of Child Language*, 11(1), 43–79.

Hart, B. and Risley, T. (1995) *Meaningful Differences in the Everyday Experience of Young American Children*. Baltimore, MD: P.H. Brookes.

Hirsh-Pasek, K., Adamson, L.B., Bakeman, R., Owen, M.T., Golinkoff, R.M., Pace, A., Yust, P.K.S. and Suma, K. (2015) The contribution of early communication quality to low-income children's language success. *Psychological Science*, 26(7), 1071–1083.

Jones, M. (2016) *Talking and Learning with Young Children*. Thousand Oaks, CA: Sage.

Karmiloff, K. and Karmiloff-Smith, A. (2002) *Pathways to Language: From Fetus to Adolescent*. Cambridge, MA: Harvard University Press.

Millard, W. and Menzies, L. (2016) *The State of Speaking in Our Schools: Oracy in English Schools*. Available at: www.researchgate.net/publication/330811980_The_State_of_Speaking_in_Our_Schools_Oracy_in_English_Schools [Accessed on 21 March 2024].

Pascal, C., Bertram, T. and Cole-Alback, A. (2017) *The Hundred Review: What Research Tells Us About Effective Pedagogic Practice and Children's Outcomes in the Reception Year.* Centre for Research in Early Childhood (CREC). Available at: http://earlyexcellence.com/wp-content/uploads/2017/05/10_100-Review_CREC_March_2017.pdf [Accessed 1 February 2024].

Pascal, C., Bertram, T. and Rouse, L. (2019) *Getting it Right in the Early Years Foundation Stage: A Review of the Evidence.* Early Education. Available at: https://early-education.org.uk/wp-content/uploads/2021/12/Getting-it-right-in-the-EYFS-Literature-Review.pdf [Accessed 1 January 2024].

Payler, J., Wood, E., Georgeson, J., Davis, G., Jarvis, P., Rose, J., Gilbert, L., Hood, P., Mitchell, H. and Chesworth, L. (2017) *BERA-TACTYC Early Childhood Research Review 2003–2017.* Available at: http://oro.open.ac.uk/50282/ [Accessed 6 March 2024].

Romeo, R.R., Leonard, J.A., Robinson, S.T., West, M.R., Mackey, A.P., Rowe, M.L. and Gabrieli, J.D.E. (2018) Beyond the 30-million-word gap: Children's conversational exposure is associated with language-related brain function. *Psychological Science*, 29(5), 700–710.

Roulstone, S., Law, J., Rush, R., Clegg, J. and Peters, T. (2011) *The Role of Language in Children's Early Educational Outcomes.* Research Brief. DFE-RB 134. London: DfE.

Siraj-Blatchford, I., Sylva, K., Muttock, S., Gilden, R. and Bell, D. (2002). *Researching Effective Pedagogy in the Early Years. Institute of Education.* University of London. Available at: https://dera.ioe.ac.uk/id/eprint/4650/1/RR356.pdf [Accessed 1 January 2024].

Snowling, M.J. and Hulme, C. (2011) Evidence-based interventions for reading and language difficulties: Creating a virtuous circle. *British Journal of Educational Psychology*, 81(1), 1–23.

Soto-Calvo, E., Simmons, F.R., Willis, C. and Adams, A.M. (2015) Identifying the cognitive predictors of early counting and calculation skills: Evidence from a longitudinal study. *Journal of Experimental Child Psychology*, 140, 16–37.

Sperry, D.E., Sperry, L.L. and Miller, P.J. (2019) Language *does* matter: But there is more to language than vocabulary and directed speech. *Child Development*, 90(3), 993–997.

Tabors, P. (1997) *One Child, Two Languages: A Guide for Preschool Educators of Children Learning English as a Second Language.* Baltimore, MD: Paul Brookes.

Tickell, C. (2011) *The Early Years: Foundations for Life, Health and Learning. An Independent Report on the Early Years Foundation Stage to Her Majesty's Government.* Available at: https://assets.publishing.service.gov.uk/media/5a7ac0ec40f0b66a2fc02915/DFE-00177-2011.pdf [Accessed 6 April 2024].

5

PERSONAL, SOCIAL AND EMOTIONAL DEVELOPMENT

> *There has never been a more important time to prioritise children's wellbeing and nurture them. This calls for us to develop a 'loving pedagogy' and speak the language of love!*
>
> Grimmer, 2020

INTRODUCTION

Children's personal, social and emotional development (PSED) has been a crucial aspect of the early years. The early years is such a joyous time of life. Staring into the eyes of a newborn baby we can never be sure how they will develop – what potential they have within them – but we know that giving them the best possible chance is everything we can do for them. Watching a child grow up, it is impossible to lay out all of the key points of development, as they are all interrelated. This chapter is going to lay out key components to PSED for children in the EYFS. Much of a child's development is a process of learning, which can be shaped by the environment. When taking a closer look at PSED, we know that children pass through many important developmental stages. The EYFS recognises that children being able to develop a sense of belonging is crucial to allowing them to gain confidence and inner strength through secure attachments with other people. The chapter will explore self-esteem, living and learning with others, emotional wellbeing and how to develop children's independence. Further take-away ideas on how to implement these within your Early Years settings will also be explored.

ATTACHMENT AND THE KEY PERSON

The EYFS requires that each child in a group setting should have a 'key person'. Sometimes we see this as a requirement to have in principle. However, the key person takes on much responsibility for the children and also works closely with their progress, communication and providing a safe and secure environment for the child. Goldschmied and Jackson (2004) introduced the term 'key person'. This term refers to a practitioner with whom the child is able to relate in a unique manner. A central component of this approach is the attachment between the young child and the practitioner.

Elfer et al. (2011) argue that it is important for every child to have one or two people who are special to them, who help them manage their day, thinking about them throughout the day. It is necessary to have a second individual available as a 'back-up' should the key individual not be available. *Birth to 5 Matters* (Early Years Coalition, 2021, p. 30) states: 'The key person helps the child to feel known, understood, cared about, and safe. The key person helps the baby or child feel confident that they are "held in mind", thought about and loved.' This experience of being cared for by reliable adults who meet their physical needs and remain attentive and playful, affectionate and thoughtful allows children to form secure attachments. Such a grounding provides a 'secure base' from which children feel confident to explore the world and form other relationships. This is backed up with the work of Peter Elfer who argues that the complex child–practitioner relationship needs a nurturing environment in which it can thrive (Elfer et al., 2011).

The key person is fundamental in being able to communicate and play an important role with ongoing relationships with parents. Early years professionals have general experience of many children and their development. Drawing upon this notion, we can help parents with many things such as: supporting children's behaviour; and having a discussion around children's health and wellbeing, including nutrition and routines.

It is essential to build up a relationship with parents as they are the advocates for their children. An important key factor to take on board here is that children have unique capabilities. Building a relationship with the family, working together in a respectful and collaborative way means that we can put the child at the centre of our practices.

There is a 'triangle of trust' (as outlined in Early Years Coalition, 2021) between the key person and the child and family (see Figure 5.1). The key person approach aims to ensure that all children and families within a setting have a special, nurturing relationship with at least one person. In the absence of a parent, the presence of a key person can provide reassurance to the child and provide parents with a point of contact when they are away from home. The availability of a key person can be ensured in a variety of ways (e.g., shared and paired care, or support partners or buddies).

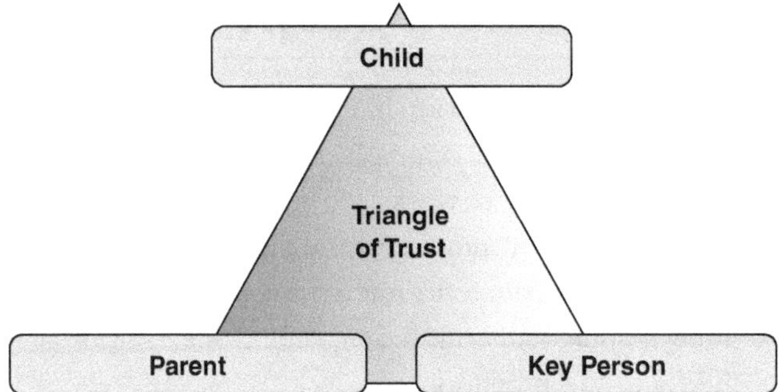

Figure 5.1 The triangle of trust, depicting the key person role

Source: Early Years Coalition (2021).

QUALITITIES OF A KEY PERSON

A key person is:

- passionate about their work and realises the value and rewards of the position;
- empathises and understands the different ways of creating a family;
- respects and appreciates the cultures, identities and diverse backgrounds of the children and families they serve;
- communicates effectively with other agencies and settings involved in the child's and family's care without making judgements;
- has a high level of education and/or extensive knowledge and understanding of, for example:
  - child development
  - attachment theory
  - self-regulation and co-regulation
  - neuroscience (brain development)
  - effective, relational pedagogy
- recognises that this is not only a professional relationship, but also a personal one that brings with it a great deal of joy as well as a great deal of challenge.

(Adapted from Early Years Coalition, 2021)

CASE STUDY 5.1

JENNET: EARLY YEARS ROOM LEADER AT A PRESCHOOL

Prior to starting at our nursery, all of our children have a home visit. This home visit allows us to determine who is best suited to be the child's key person. To have this discussion, we always go to the home in pairs. It is also easier for the parents since they have already met one of us. As soon as the child starts, we give the family an information book that tells them all about their key person and what to expect. From the outset, it is clear what phone number to call, what email address to use and what hours they are available to be contacted. As we are usually in ratio, it can be difficult at times, but we do try to make sure that we have one hour a week where we can be available to the families.

As a result, we will be able to have discussions with them over the phone or face-to-face about things that they may be struggling with at home, and also build on relationships with the parents and get to know the children in depth. Our conversations usually start with the child's unique abilities and the trust they build with you as a professional. Laughter, joy and tears are part of the experience, but it is a safe place where parents feel confident working with us, knowing that we care as much about their children as they do.

REFLECTION 5.1

1. How do you set out your key person approach?
2. Do you have a home visit system similar to Jennet?
3. Putting time aside for families is a crucial opportunity to build on aspects of the key person role. Could this be applied within your setting?

CHILDREN'S EMOTIONS

When a baby is born, they have little ability to self-regulate; however, from infancy, parents and other primary caregivers are able to assist the child in learning through a process called co-regulation. A parent or primary caregiver can help an infant or young child become calmer and more regulated by using their voice, movements, affects, gestures and intonations. In the course of growing up, babies who have a high degree of co-regulation during stressful situations, such as when they are struggling with strong feelings, are able to internalise and conceptualise strategies for self-regulation and self-soothing.

> Developing self-regulation, like many elements of development and learning, is not something children do by themselves. It is a process that grows out of attuned relationships where the caregiver and baby or child are closely attentive to each other and engage in sensitive, responsive exchanges.
>
> (Early Years Coalition, 2021, p. 20)

Co-regulation – our attuned, attentive and loving interactions with children – is crucial to children's emotional development and ultimately contributes to their self-regulation skills developing over time. A co-regulation relationship is a warm interaction between an adult and a child (or even between adults!), in which adults assist children in understanding their feelings and behaviour. In order for co-regulation to be effective, it must be tender, intentional and focused. As early childhood practitioners, we are responsible for paying close attention to children's emotional cues, understanding their body language, and responding quickly, consistently and sensitively to these cues. Giving the right amount of support at the right time is an important aspect of co-regulation's complexity. It is important to be prompt and consistent.

Children will develop self-regulation skills when a pedagogy includes co-regulation strategies. Three basic strategies for co-regulation have been identified by researchers:

- establish a warm, responsive relationship in which children feel respected, comfortable and supported in times of stress as well as confident that they are well taken care of;
- provide an environment that makes self-regulation manageable, is structured in a predictable manner and is physically and emotionally safe for children to explore and take risks without unnecessary stress;
- provide frequent opportunities to practise self-regulation skills and scaffolding to support children to learn the key components of these skills.

Managing one's own mental processes, including cognitive strategies, emotions, social skills and motivations, is referred to as self-regulation. A range of academic and 'soft' or '21st-century' skills development is most strongly predicted through early childhood into early adulthood by these abilities, which develop most rapidly in young children during their first seven years.

Children who achieve a high level of self-regulation during the early years are more likely to:

- be able to cope with school and make a good start in learning to read and write;
- be able to make and maintain friendships;
- in the short and long term, be able to achieve a high level of academic achievement by becoming effective learners;
- develop a strong sense of self-efficacy, i.e. belief that they are capable of learning, understanding, or solving problems, or developing abilities, if they work hard and persevere;
- maintain a high level of emotional wellbeing.

Love and nurture has a place to support PSED. As Bradbury and Grimmer (2024) explore, the concept of nurturing children implies caring for them throughout their development over time. In our children, we might nurture curiosity, nurture kindness, or nurture creativity, which means we encourage our children to cultivate these virtues or dispositions. The act of nurturing someone entails caring deeply for them and assisting them in their growth and development. Our early childhood programme focuses primarily on nurturing children in this sense. This is closely related to the concept of loving children. Nurturing a child is essential to loving them, since real love is active and is concerned for their wellbeing. The combination of love and nurture seems to be a very natural one and links well to emotional and social development.

Connecting with children's emotions is an important aspect of developing them as confident and competent learners. The ELGs are there as a guide. There are many which relate to PSED and focus on the child's needs to foster a positive relationship in social and emotional development; ELGs describe the expected level in this.

REFLECTION 5.2

- An important part of self-regulation is the development of children's ability to regulate their emotions, thoughts and behaviours, thereby enabling them to act in a positive manner towards achieving their goals.
- The concept of self-regulation emerges from the concept of co-regulation, in which adults and children work together towards a common purpose, including ways to resolve upsets brought about by stress and return to a state of balance.
- Both cognitive and emotional self-regulation are essential for behavioural self-regulation in the Early Years.
- The development of self-regulation skills can be achieved through a pedagogy that incorporates co-regulation strategies.

RELATIONSHIPS

Neuroscientific evidence and educational theory support the importance of attachments in early childhood (Bowlby, 1969; Gerhardt, 2004; Music, 2017; Zeedyk, 2013), but, in simpler terms, this refers to relationships. Read states that 'we now know through advances and research on brain development that close, loving, and intimate relationships are the key to emotional wellbeing, good mental health, and future success' (Read, 2014, p. 3). We can build secure attachments and nurture children when we keep relationships at the forefront of our practice (Bradbury and Grimmer, 2024). Relationship-building requires the adult to be available to the child on an emotional and physical level, attentive to their needs and attuned to their interests (Grimmer, 2021). In Noddings' (2002) description of this 'attentive love', an educator notices a child appearing uncomfortable and asks, 'Do you need a nappy change?' It involves engaging in respectful interactions with a child, responding to their needs, context, wants and emotions based on your knowledge of them.

BUILDING ON PSED THROUGH THE CONCEPT OF PLAY, LOVE AND NURTURE

Children benefit from play. The act of playing is a natural and enjoyable means of keeping children active, healthy and happy. Children and young people benefit from play that is freely chosen for their health and development. A variety of unstructured play opportunities must be provided to children from birth in order for them to be able to have good physical and mental health and to learn life skills (Play England, 2020). Friedrich Froebel, one of early childhood's pioneers, stated:

> I wanted to educate people to be free, to think, to action for themselves.
>
> (Froebel in Lilley, 1967, p. 41)

Figure 5.2 Depiction of a child feeling loved within their early years setting, becoming empowered and ready to learn and play

Note: Developed by Aaron Bradbury. See Grimmer (2022).

In Froebel's view, the child has the right to determine their own actions based on the laws and demands of the play in which they are participating. Through this process, the child can develop a sense of independence and autonomy (Froebel in Liebschner, 1992). According to Froebel, free play helps children make choices, solve problems and develop their own interests and talents. Froebel's views on free play are consistent with those of Grimmer (2021), who asserts that children must feel secure and free in their learning environment in order to play and learn freely. As depicted in Figure 5.2, the child is confident and empowered within their learning environment as they explore their surroundings.

Play has so many benefits – it is varied and is vital for children within the EYFS. Play for social and emotional development has the following benefits to young children.

- *Social development*: The development of empathy involves noticing social cues, listening and taking another person's perspective when playing with others. In addition to sharing ideas and expressing feelings, social play requires children to negotiate and reach a compromise while expressing their feelings.
- *Emotional development*: Children learn self-regulation through social and guided play, in which they follow norms and pay attention while experiencing emotions such as anticipation and frustration. Additionally, play teaches children how to establish and change rules, and when to lead and when to follow.

FOSTERING INDEPENDENT THINKERS

An early childhood professional's most ambitious goal is to see children develop into independent thinkers. Children's thinking is influenced by strong support, as illustrated by Sue Gerhardt in her book *Why Love Matters* (2004), and Bradbury and Grimmer in their book *Love and Nurture in the Early Years* (2024). An early childhood professional must place more emphasis on adopting opportunities from professional insights in their day-to-day work, as well as listening to the voice of the child.

Children have the opportunity to share their thoughts with us when they are listened to. In our early childhood sector, every professional who works with children from birth to five and older should ensure that the child's voice is heard, considered and taken into account. It is more successful to obtain a child's views when there is a meaningful engagement and interaction with that child. From a professional perspective, this approach is crucial when it comes to relating to children as individuals and enabling them to become active social agents in their decision-making processes.

To gain the voice of the child, it is imperative that a strong relationship is developed with the child, as well as a position of trust where the child can express their opinions. It is essential that the child is aware of their right to be heard and that they can participate in decisions that affect them.

We, as early childhood professionals, must be able to understand the values and backgrounds of the child, their situation, their cultural position and their unique needs. It is also important to consider their story: what is their purpose in coming to your Early Years setting? It is important to maintain a partnership with parents throughout the process. To achieve key learning and developmental outcomes and to achieve the *characteristics of effective learning*, it is imperative to gain the voice of the child. There are strong connections between British values, democracy, diversity and equality.

Any assessment practice should incorporate the voice of the child. If this is well structured and supported by the professionals, children can become involved in thinking about their own learning and development. It is highly valued to listen to the views of children and to respect their rights. In addition to children who speak English as an additional language, those with speech or developmental delays or disabilities also may not be able to communicate verbally. However, they can express their interests in other ways – by using gestures, actions, body language, signing, or by drawing and painting – to demonstrate their likes and dislikes.

Ways of gaining the voice of the child for children who have development or speech delays include:

- Makaton signing
- drawing/painting
- role play
- gestures
- voice dissatisfaction – through sounds
- body language
- observation.

The process of gaining the child's voice should be a daily one within your practice. In spite of this, we sometimes take for granted the daily communication that we have with children. Every interaction with children in your care should be viewed as communication, as part of telling and building a story about that child.

CASE STUDY 5.2

EVIE

Evie is three. This morning is her first day at nursery. Her key worker Bashir went to the house to see Evie and her mum Kate a couple of weeks ago.

Evie is a child who finds new situations difficult, but Kate knows that she will enjoy her nursery experience and thinks that being with other children will be positive for her. Kate works part time and Evie has been looked after by her grandmother.

Evie communicates well, plays with certain toys such as cars and occasionally the fluffy doll, and is able to show her likes and dislikes. She particularly showed this on her home visit from the nursery where she didn't want to play with the jigsaws; instead she wanted to play with the cars in the see-through bag.

Evie was being dropped at nursery early today, mainly due to mum, Kate, having to start work at 9am. Evie hasn't been cared for before by someone other than her family members. Kate has never really wanted her to be looked after by another person. However, the time has come, and Evie is at the nursery door. Bashir, her key worker, welcomes Evie and Kate into the nursery. Evie holds onto Kate's hand and walks into the preschool room. There are some children there already; Evie goes over to the carpet area and Kate leaves. Bashir sits with Evie and some children come over and start talking to Evie, showing her what they are currently playing with. Evie quickly starts to look at her surroundings, playing with the blocks and then moving on to the paints. Some children say to Bashir that Evie isn't saying anything to them or isn't playing with them all the time. Evie has been spending time on her own and watches the children. She sits on the chair by the paints and isn't speaking to the other children, but does communicate in her own way. Bashir quickly goes and reassures Evie – after all, it's such a new environment; Evie has never been in this environment before. She isn't distressed, but Bashir can feel that she isn't comfortable either, due to the new surroundings and that she is missing her comfort of home.

In this case study, we have not attempted to detail too much of a situation, other than to give you a brief description of a child named Evie's first day. There are many aspects of Evie's day that you can relate to.

REFLECTION 5.3

Based on the case study above, how would you gain the perspective of Evie? What are her likes and dislikes?

When Evie first arrived, what did she gravitate towards and what would Bashir be doing constantly?

Evie has met Bashir before, so she may feel comfortable going into his preschool room. Evie, however, is assessing her current situation, regulating what is happening around her – noises, new experiences, regulating the positions of the other children – and gaining confidence within her new social environment. The key to success here is communication, but does it have to be verbal? Bashir was able to observe her body language and facial expressions. Additionally, I have not attributed a particular characteristic of communication difficulty to Evie, as this is the child's situation.

REFLECTION 5.4

- What would you do?
- How would you approach it?
- What advice would you give to Bashir?

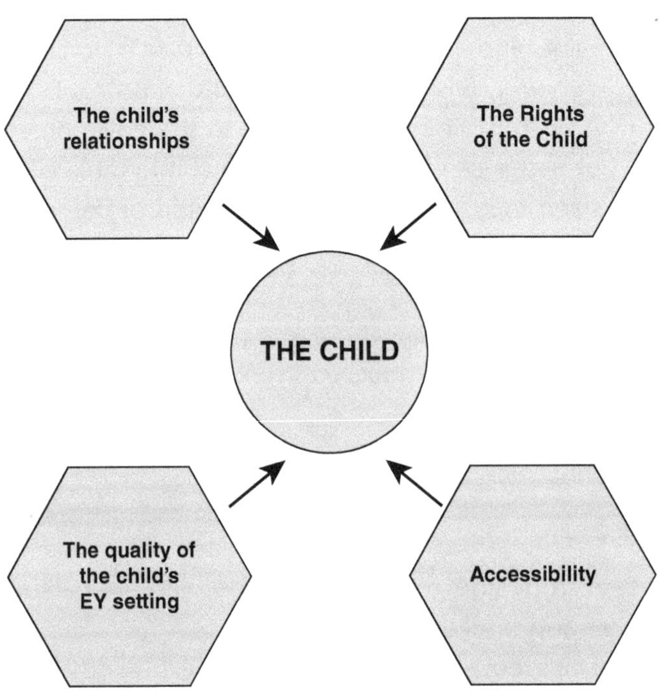

Figure 5.3 Putting the child at the centre of PSED: the voice of the child in context

It is important to keep the child at the centre of all of our decisions, to recognise their wishes and feelings, as well as ensuring that we fully understand them. Figure 5.3 illustrates the need for the child to be positioned at the centre of all of our decisions. By focusing on the child, their voice is heard, they can understand their rights and they can also understand what is being asked of them. Therefore, practice is based on their needs and experiences. Furthermore, it is important to recognise young children first and foremost as citizens if we are to understand their own perspectives on partnership (Pascal and Bertram, 2009). To fully embed the voice of the child in our setting, practitioners need to accept that children require agency, paying close attention to the child with respect. Consequently, it is important that practitioners consider empowerment and the use of professional skills through observation in order to gain the child's voice.

KEY POINTS OF THE CHAPTER

Teachers and Early Years professionals approach the goal of PSED to help children develop positive self-images, respect for others, social skills, emotional wellbeing and to foster a positive attitude towards learning. All of these are essential for developing children and ensuring that they are at the centre of our practices.

PSED for children in the EYFS involves:

- the development of confidence and independence;
- getting along with others and making friends;
- developing a sense of right and wrong;
- emotional self-regulation;
- understanding their own feelings as well as those of others;
- having a positive self-image;
- having a keen interest in, excitement about and motivation for their play and learning;
- developing a sense of self-respect;
- learning to respect the cultures and beliefs of others as well as their own.

REFERENCES

Bowlby, J. (1969) *Attachment and Loss: Volume 1. Attachment.* New York: Basic Books.

Bradbury, A. and Grimmer, T. (2024) *Love and Nurture in the Early Years.* London: Learning Matters.

Early Years Coalition (2021) *Birth to 5 Matters Non-statutory Guidance to the Early Years Foundation Stage*. Available at: https://birthto5matters.org.uk/wp-content/uploads/2021/03/Birthto5Matters-download.pdf [Accessed 1 January 2024].

Elfer, P., Goldschmied, E. and Selleck, D. (2011) *Key Persons in the Early Years*. London: David Fulton.

Gerhardt, S. (2004) *Why Love Matters: How Affection Shapes a Baby's Brain*. Hove: Brunner-Routledge.

Goldschmied, E. and Jackson, S. (2004) *People Under Three: Young Children in Day Care*. London: Psychology Press.

Grimmer, T. (2020) *10 Top Tips for Developing a 'Loving Pedagogy' in the Early Years*. Available at: https://kinderly.co.uk/2020/08/18/10-top-tips-for-developing-a-loving-pedagogy-in-early-years/ [Accessed 1 February 2024].

Grimmer, T. (2021) *Developing a Loving Pedagogy in the Early Years: How Love Fits with Professional Practice*. London: Routledge.

Liebschner, J. (1992) *A Child's Work: Freedom and Guidance in Froebel's Educational Theory and Practice*. Cambridge: Lutterworth Press.

Lilley, I. (1967) *Friedrich Froebel: A Selection from his Writings*. Cambridge: Cambridge University Press.

Music, G. (2017) *Nurturing Natures: Attachment and Children's Emotional, Sociocultural and Brain Development*. London: Routledge.

Noddings, N. (2002) *Starting at Home: Caring and Social Policy*. London: University of California Press.

Pascal, C. and Bertram, T. (2009) Listening to young citizens: The struggle to make real a participatory paradigm in research with young children. *European Early Childhood Education Research Journal*, 17(2), 249–262.

Play England (2020) *Charter for Play*. Available at: www.playengland.org.uk/charter-for-play [Accessed 1 January 2024].

Read, V. (2014) *Developing Attachment in Early Years Settings: Nurturing Secure Relationships from Birth to Five Years* (2nd edn). London: Routledge.

Zeedyk, S. (2013) *Sabre Tooth Tigers and Teddy Bears: The Connected Baby Guide to Understanding Attachment*. Dundee: Suzanne Zeedyk.

6

PHYSICAL DEVELOPMENT

When there is motor and physical activity, you can see a more important kind of education, a kind of education that takes the force of life into account. This education is not driven by its own wisdom, but by another superior wisdom which lays down the law that, if we do not take the vital force into account, we miss the best part of education.

Maria Montessori, 1946

INTRODUCTION

Helen Battelley describes physical development as the 'poor relation of the prime areas' and it can be perceived as sometimes being side-lined, particularly as children move towards formal schooling at the end of the Foundation Stage. Battelley (2021) also argues that movement is our first language and first form of communication with the outside world. I am inclined to agree with her sentiments here.

On returning to school after the Covid lockdown, Ofsted found that in preschool and nursery settings:

> Some providers said that they continued to focus on children's physical development. Providers were more focused on developing children's gross motor skills. They knew that some children did not have access to outdoor space during lockdowns and, even where they did, they were limited to a smaller variety of outdoor spaces. Some providers adapted their outdoor play areas and were teaching children to use a greater variety

> of play equipment outside, for example larger slides, more climbing equipment, bikes, and sand and water play areas.
>
> Some providers, specifically those in more deprived areas, had spent more funding than they would have pre-pandemic for this, as they recognised that these opportunities may be limited for children at home.
>
> (Ofsted, 2021)

In comparison to their findings in schools:

> Many schools identified that pupils had missed out on PE and general physical activity. Leaders said that some pupils have returned to school unfit, more overweight and lacking physical resilience and stamina. No schools inspected had chosen to increase the amount of physical activity for children.
>
> (Ofsted, 2021)

These responses after the 2020 lockdown can't be taken at face value as a reflection of the picture across all schools and settings, but it is interesting to note the difference in responses of different parts of the sector to the impact of lockdown.

Over the last few years there has been an increasing focus on cognitive development, with cognitive load theory dominating much of the discussion around children's learning. These discussions have shaped DfE guidance and Ofsted frameworks. What we know is that we can't separate the brain from the body and, for young children in particular, physical development is vital to their learning.

During the first few years of life children are undergoing rapid development. In early infanthood we focus on many of the physical milestones – the first time a baby holds up their own head, sits up unaided, crawls and walks are all key milestones that parents and carers celebrate. Children are learning by constantly moving, they are exploring their world and their space within it, initially through reaching, grasping objects and mouthing them, eventually crawling, walking and climbing. Young children are constantly on the move. At the same time as the obvious physical changes are happening to the child's body, there are changes taking place in the child's brain architecture. Our brain is at its most 'plastic', it is most susceptible to learning in the first few years of life. Neuronal connections are being made which change the brain's architecture; by 36 months a child's brain is as complex as it will ever be (Shore, 2003). In the first six years synapses are forming connections, as children grow and develop some of these connections become hardwired and others are lost. This process is often referred to as blooming and pruning. When connections are not used, they are lost or 'pruned'. Children who do not have sufficient opportunities to move and be active may lose some of the synapses responsible for physical activity. In fact, NHS guidelines around movement in young children are very clear, young children should not be sitting still for long periods of time. The NHS recommends that young children under five should be active for at least 180 minutes per day, at least 60 of which should involve them getting out of breath and that children aged five to 18 should take part in a variety of types and intensities of physical activity across the week to develop movement skills, muscles and bones and reduce the time spent sitting or lying down. They recommend that children in this age group should aim for 60 minutes of moderate or intense activity every day.

We know that today's children spend much less time outside than their counterparts 50 years ago. A 2016 study found that more than one in nine children had not set foot in a park, forest, beach or any other natural environment in the last 12 months (Natural England, 2016). According to a recent Teacher Tapp survey, schools in areas of deprivation have shorter breaks, meaning children from disadvantaged backgrounds are getting less time to move at school. These children may also have less access to safe outdoor spaces than their more affluent peers.

A recent report from Kindred identified issues around children not being able to sit still, dress independently, toilet independently or hold a pencil when starting school. These were all considered aspects of 'school readiness' in their survey and all require attention to children's physical development needs: 83 per cent of respondents to the survey cited children's inability to sit still as having a major or moderate impact on the progress of the whole class; 77 per cent identified toileting needs as having a major or moderate impact on the progress of the whole class; and 46 per cent of those surveyed had allocated more time or staff to deal with physical care in Reception.

INFLUENCES ON CHILDREN'S PHYSICAL DEVELOPMENT

We know that Ofsted reported that providers and schools recognised the impact of the first and subsequent lockdowns on children's physical development. This will have impacted children from different socio-economic backgrounds differently. Some children will have spent time in their gardens, possibly with carers who had more time to give them than usual because they were not working from home. Whereas other children who didn't have access to gardens could not access play areas as these were closed. Their early physical development is likely to have been impacted by these restrictions.

The growing trend in some societies towards a sedentary lifestyle has been the subject of much discussion for many years and the increase of screen time for all members of society, but particularly under-18s, has been the subject of much debate.

According to the Centre for Disease Control, the average daily screen time for an eight-year-old is 9 hours per day (Binns, 2023). This is a worrying statistic. There are fewer statistics available for children under eight but we know that under-threes have access to mobile devices and tablets. Parental attitudes towards technology play a significant part in the amount of time children access screens (O'Connor and Fotakopoulou, 2016).

CASE STUDY 6.1

THE IMPACT OF A NEW PHONICS SCHEME

Table 6.1 Timetable taken from a school implementing a DfE-accredited phonics scheme, September 2021

Day	8.50–9	9–9.45	9.45–10.45	10.45–11.25	11.25–11.45	11.45–12	12–1.15	1.15–1.40	1.45 – 2.50	2.50–3.15
Monday	Self-reg	Phonics	Reading groups	CP+ individual readers	Maths	Story time	L	Topic/Curriculum input	Catch-up phonics CP (outdoors if sufficient staff)	Story time
Tuesday	Self-reg	Phonics	Reading groups	CP+ individual readers	Maths	Story time	U	PE (until 2pm)	Catch-up phonics CP (outdoors if sufficient staff)	Story time
Wednesday	Self-reg	Phonics	Reading groups	CP+ individual readers	Maths	Story time	N	Topic/Curriculum input	Catch-up phonics CP (outdoors if sufficient staff)	Story time
Thursday	Self-reg	Phonics	Reading groups	CP +individual readers	Maths	Story time	C	Topic/Curriculum input	Catch-up phonics CP (outdoors if sufficient staff)	Story time
Friday	Self-reg	Phonics	Reading groups	CP +individual readers	Maths	Story time	H	Topic/Curriculum input	Continuous provision	Story time

CONTEXT

The school had just adopted one of the government-accredited phonics schemes. The criteria for accreditation include meeting or exceeding the expectations of the EYFS and National Curriculum. This particular scheme exceeds the expectations and children progress through the scheme at a very fast pace. There are many 'keep up, not catch up' sessions for children who are struggling to keep up with the programme.

The school is an inner-city school in an area of significant deprivation, which has been impacted by Covid and at this time was still operating a bubble system due to the high levels of Covid in the local community – 77 per cent of the cohort are new to learning English and many are new to the UK.

The children were struggling to keep up with the pace of the phonics programme, so the majority of the children were in 'keep up' sessions. This meant that staffing in the provision was reduced, with the teacher and TA in each class both leading keep-up groups. This reduces supervision so the children could not access the outdoors until the afternoon and sometimes this was not possible due to catch-up sessions.

Although it is difficult to determine the precise amount of time children spend looking at screens, Palaiologou (2014) found that 60 per cent of children under three had access to digital technology such as tablets. Since most parents estimate that screen usage has increased since the pandemic, we might assume that access and the amount of time spent on technology has increased. While technology itself is not a bad thing, the amount of time children spend sitting still to use it will have impacted on their physical development.

What we do know is that, according to DfE statistics in 2021, 9.3 per cent of Reception-age children were obese and 12.1 per cent of Reception-age children were overweight. Children who are overweight at five have a 30 per cent chance of returning to a healthy weight and a 30 per cent chance of becoming obese by age 11. Children who are obese at five have a 70 per cent chance of becoming obese by 11. Once established, obesity is challenging to reverse and approximately 60–85 per cent of children with obesity remain obese in adulthood, significantly increasing their risks of future ill health. While these statistics are based on body mass index, which is not without flaws as it doesn't take into account muscle mass so keen sports people can sometimes fall within the 'overweight' band, the figures should not be ignored. We know that obesity increases the chances of significant health issues which can impact on quality of life and life span. We need to make sure that movement is part of our everyday practice in Early Years.

Young children want to move, in fact they often struggle to keep still. This is because they are still discovering what their bodies can do and finding out about the space they take up in the world. It is important to reflect on how much time is spent over the course of the day and the week in your setting on allowing children to move.

The increasing impact of 'top down' pressure, leading to the 'schoolification' of some Early Years settings has meant that some children's opportunities for physical development have become extremely restricted, but there is significant research (Goddard-Blythe, 2010; O'Connor and Daly, 2012; Grissmer et al., 2016) to show that motor skills in early childhood are significant predictors of achievement in reading and mathematics at primary school.

REFLECTION 6.1

How much time is spent on physical development in this class?

When is the first time a child can get out of breath in the setting?

Are the children getting their recommended amount of physical activity per day?

How long would a child who was in keep-up sessions spend sitting still each day?

Is this a broad and balanced curriculum?

Is it equitable? Some children (those who are able to keep up with the scheme) have more time to play and move than others.

How could we review practice to ensure that all children have access to adequate physical development opportunities?

Obviously, this is an extreme example, but it is a useful provocation. We know that being literate matters, but how far should we tip the balance in the curriculum towards schemes that are aimed at 'broadly typical' children when a significant number are struggling to keep up?

It is worth reflecting on your own timetable and asking yourself how much time is spent on this key prime area. It is also important to note that there are many physical prerequisites to becoming literate.

PHYSICAL DEVELOPMENT AND ITS IMPACT ON WIDER LEARNING

It's helpful to read this chapter in conjunction with Chapters 4, 7, 9 and 10, as they are closely interconnected. There is extensive research which shows that supporting children's gross and fine motor control and physical development is a key factor in early learning. The evidence indicates strongly that good physical development is vital to cognitive development and is an essential part of children's general wellbeing, which has a significant impact on long-term outcomes (Pascal et al., 2019).

Perhaps the one area of physical development that is given lots of attention is fine motor control. Many settings and schools incorporate fine motor activities and specific teaching to develop fine motor skills. While this is important, fine motor control is directly linked to gross motor development. Our bodies develop proximally to distally, we gain control of the parts closest to our core first. It makes sense to ensure that we have the correct emphasis on gross motor development alongside fine motor skills.

Young children start to gain control of their core in early infanthood. Newborns have primary reflexes to enable them to root, grasp, startle and turn to a familiar voice. We notice when the baby rolls over, holds their head up, is able to sit unaided as their muscles and skeleton begin to develop and the baby begins to interact more with their environment. As their core muscles and strength develop, they become more coordinated learning to stretch and reach, to shuffle, crawl and eventually to walk. These physical skills are important in their own right but there is a wealth of research evidence to show that they also impact on the child's ability to learn and express their learning. 'Throughout life movement acts as a primary medium through which information is derived from the senses is integrated, and knowledge of the world is expressed' (Goddard-Blythe, 2011, p. 131).

PHYSICAL ASPECTS OF EARLY LITERACY

In our case study, the focus on becoming literate was leading to diminished opportunities for children to move. However, there are many physical prerequisites to early literacy.

We have already talked about the impact of gross motor skills on developing fine motor skills which are necessary to manipulate tools such as pencils, but there are many aspects of physical development which need to be taken into consideration if we are to support children with their early reading and writing.

Children need to have well-developed balance and postural control in order to be able to write. This comes from having good gross motor control and is essential if we are to ask children to sit still. Johnson (2007) argues that children need to have a strong sense of balance both when moving and sitting still. Balance is controlled by our vestibular system; this provides information to our brain about motion and orientation. McPhillips et al. (2000) noted that children who experience difficulties with reading also experience difficulties with balance and motor control (Payler et al., 2017).

Proprioception, the process of knowing where our bodies are in the space we occupy, is something which is second nature to most adults but is still developing in young children. It is extremely challenging to control your body when you don't quite know whereabouts all of it is! We develop both balance and proprioception by moving. Children do not learn to sit still by sitting still, they need to develop these skills by climbing, crawling, running, spinning, negotiating large outdoor spaces and lifting heavy objects. Sitting still for long periods of time is challenging. The younger the child the more challenging this is, and this will place a cognitive load on the child as their focus shifts from what adults are saying to controlling their bodies in order to keep still.

There are links between balance, eye movements, visual perception, proprioception and literacy skills. Eye movements and visual perception are linked to balance (Goddard-Blythe, 2000) and reading and writing are both motor skills which require well-established postural control and control of the eyes, tongue, lips and mouth. Johnson (2014) argues that when proprioception is fully developed children can look at letters and use their eyes to track the direction of lines and curves, they are then able to form accurate mental images from this information.

Goddard-Blythe (2000) argues that greater attention should be given to the development of gross motor skills when considering whether children are ready for the demands of formal schooling. She cites a number of key skills which would indicate whether a child is ready.

CROSSING THE MIDLINE: BILATERAL INTEGRATION

If we imagine there is a line running down the centre of the body separating left from right, children's ability to carry out simple tasks requires the ability to cross the midline. Using a pencil, brushing hair, playing a game with a ball or a bat and ball all require good communication between the left- and right-hand side of the brain. This develops through observable stages: young children will move their hands symmetrically to reach out; crawling requires reciprocal movement – what happens on one side of the body is repeated on the other, the next stage involves both sides of the body working together to perform complementary tasks; one hand holding the paper while the other makes marks, for example. Finally, when a child is able to cross their midline their hand can reach over to the other side of the body. So, the left hand can complete tasks on the right side of the body and vice versa. At this point children may start to develop a dominant hand. Crossing the midline is an important skill for reading and writing, as children need to be able to track left to right (O'Connor and Daly, 2016).

SENSORY AWARENESS AND INTEGRATION

Children's ability to receive and respond to information gathered through their senses as well as their interoception (being able to respond to their internal messages such as hunger, pain, emotions, etc.) and internal vestibular and proprioception shapes their neural pathways. The way we make sense of the world around us from babyhood onwards involves exploring it with all of these senses (O'Connor and Daly, 2016). Young children need rich sensorimotor experiences in order to make sense of their world and their place in it. Sensory integration affects how the child understands, responds to and interprets sensory information (Connell and McCarthy, 2014).

NEURO-MOTOR INTEGRATION

Goddard-Blythe identifies this area as an indicator of readiness to learn. She argues that a significant number of children retain primary reflexes which should start to diminish at around six months as the child develops and matures physically.

Blythe and Hyland (2016) found differences in early development in children who had reading, writing and copying difficulties in comparison to groups without difficulties. They noted that there were a range of significant physical factors including: later learning to walk, talk, ride a bicycle, catch a ball, fasten buttons, tying shoelaces.

Factors which impacted on children's development of phonological skills were: being later learning to talk, a history of more frequent ear, nose and throat infections in the first three years of life and hypersensitivity to sounds by the age of seven.

Goddard-Blythe noted that the common factor among many children was that none had passed through the developmental stage of crawling on their tummy or creeping on hands and knees. While this in itself is not an indicator of future learning difficulties, Goddard-Blythe noted that to be able to crawl and creep a child needs to have independent use of upper and lower right and left sections of the body and head control and that at this stage children start to synchronise their vision, balance and proprioception, and to further develop hand–eye coordination at a similar visual distance to the one they will use when reading in later life.

BACK TO HANDWRITING

The obsession in England with a tripod grip, which now forms part of the early learning goals for fine motor development, despite being impossible and uncomfortable for some children depending on their age and stage of physical development, can have a detrimental impact on writing. Children who are constantly corrected may be put off writing and may just need more time for their bones and muscles to mature in order to be ready to use this grip. Occupational therapists agree that this typically happens between the ages of 4.5 to six years old, but can vary depending on the child. Young children's bones are still developing up to the age of 19 through a process called ossification, where hormones are released which turn the cartilage in their hands to bones. I share this image with teachers to illustrate how this can impact on children's ability to write.

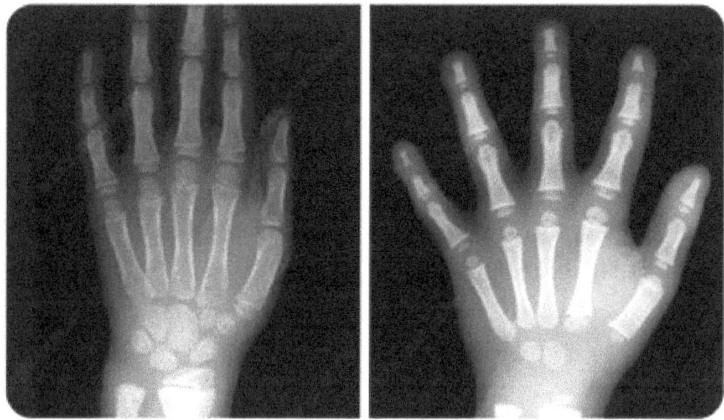

Figure 6.1 X-rays of children's hands at different stages of development

On the left of Figure 6.1 we can see an x-ray of the hand of a child aged around seven to eight, on the right an x-ray of the hand of a three- to four-year-old.

The process of ossification doesn't follow the same timeline for all children; some children will have the endocrinal release that changes the cartilage to bone before others. But we can't speed it up. This doesn't mean we shouldn't encourage children to write, but we need to acknowledge that writing is not easy and requires tremendous effort. We need to make it irresistible to young children and provide the right tools for them.

Some children never develop a tripod grip but have beautiful handwriting. The key is to ensure that whatever grip the child uses is comfortable so that they can write at length without becoming uncomfortable. Some adults focus so much on the tripod grip that they fail to notice that children don't have the necessary core or shoulder girdle strength to produce neat writing. The tripod grip is present, but the handwriting is untidy and the child may become quickly fatigued. It is essential that those working to develop children's writing understand the importance of all aspects of physical development when supporting children to write.

REFLECTION 6.2

How much time are children physically active in your setting?

When do they get out of breath?

Are there opportunities for them to climb, balance, jump, run, crawl, transport heavy items, hang from things, build their upper body and shoulder girdle strength?

Is physical activity given the same status as the other prime areas in your setting?

Given what we know about the importance of physical development and its impact on all other learning, how can we ensure that those who don't work in Early Years understand its importance?

KEY POINTS OF THE CHAPTER

It is vital that we ensure that physical development is given the same status as the other prime areas. Not only is physical development important for health, but also it impacts on our cognitive development as well as our general wellbeing which is vital for healthy development from birth (Pascal et al., 2019). It is impossible to develop the brain separately from the body and if we don't value both gross and fine motor skills, we are missing essential opportunities to support young children's learning.

REFERENCES

Battelley, H. (2021) How does an intervention strategy around physical activity and movement influence parent/carers' perceptions of early childhood movement play? MA, Birmingham City University. Available at: www.crec.co.uk/research-paper-archive/ [Accessed 1 March 2024].

Binns, R. (2023) Screen time statistics 2024. *Independent*. Available at: www.independent.co.uk/advisor/vpn/screen-time-statistics#:~:text=According%20to%20The%20Centers%20for%20Disease%20Control%20and,to%2014-year-olds%207.5%20hours%20for%2015-%20to%2018-year-olds [Accessed 3 May 2024].

Blythe, S. and Hyland, D. (2016) Screening for neurological dysfunction in the specific learning difficulty child. *Occupational Therapy: The Official Journal of the Association of Occupational Therapists*, 61(10), 459–464.

Connell, G. and McCarthy, C. (2014) *A Moving Child is a Learning Child: How the Body Teaches the Brain to Think (Birth to Age 7)*. Minneapolis, MN: Free Spirit.

Department for Education (DfE) (2021) *Self Assessment Form: DfE Validation of Systematic Synthetic Phonics (SSP) Programmes*. Available at: https://view.officeapps.live.com/op/view.aspx?src=https%3A%2F%2Fassets.publishing.service.gov.uk%2Fmedia%2F6065d0848fa8f515aa902c44%2FSelf_Assessment_Form_SSP.odt&wdOrigin=BROWSELINK [Accessed 21 March 2024].

Goddard-Blythe, S. (2000) Early learning in the balance: Priming the first ABC. *Support for Learning*, 15(4), 154–158.

Goddard-Blythe, S. (2011) Physical foundations for learning. In R. House, *Too Much, Too Soon? Early Learning and the Erosion of Childhood*. Stroud: Hawthorn.

Goddard-Blythe, S. (2012) *Assessing Neuromotor Readiness for Learning: The INPP Developmental Screening Test and School Intervention Programme*. Malden, MA: John Wiley.

Grissmer, D., Grimm, K.J., Aiyer, S.M., Murrah, W.M. and Steele, J.S. (2010) Fine motor skills and early comprehension of the world: Two new school readiness indicators. *Developmental Psychology*, 46(5), 1008–1017.

Johnson, S. (2007) A developmental approach looking at the relationship of children's foundational neurological pathways to their higher capacities for learning. *You and Your Child's Health*. Available at: www.youandyourchildshealth.org/youandyourchildshealth/articles/teaching%20our%20children.html [Accessed 8 April 2024].

Johnson, S. (2014) *Teaching Our Children to Write, Read and Spell*. Available at: https://sthelenacoop.org/wp-content/uploads/2020/05/Teaching-Your-Child-to-Read-Write-Spell.pdf [Accessed 1 March 2024].

Montessori, M. (1946) *The 1946 London Lectures*. Available at: https://montessori150.org/maria-montessori/montessori-books/1946-london-lectures [Accessed 2 January 2024].

McPhillips, M., Hepper, P. and Mulhern, G. (2000) Effects of replicating primary-reflex movements on specific reading difficulties in children: A randomised, double-blind, controlled trial. *The Lancet*, 355(9203), 537–541.

Natural England (2016) *Monitor of Engagement with the Natural Environment: A Pilot to Develop an Indicator of Visits to the Natural Environment by Children (NECR208)*. Available at: https://publications.naturalengland.org.uk/publication/5286590942281728 [Accessed 6 January 2024].

O'Connor, A. and Daly, A. (2016) *Understanding Physical Development in the Early Years: Linking Bodies and Minds*. London: Routledge.

O'Connor, J. and Fotakopoulou, O. (2016) A threat to childhood innocence or the future of learning? Parents' perspectives on the use of touch-screen technology by 0–3-year-olds in the UK. *Contemporary Issues in Early Childhood*, 17(2), 235–247.

Ofsted (2021) *Education Recovery in Schools: Autumn 2021*. Available at: www.gov.uk/government/publications/education-recovery-in-schools-autumn-2021/education-recovery-in-schools-autumn-2021 [Accessed 5 May 2024].

Palaiologou, I. (2014) Children under five and digital technologies: Implications for Early Years pedagogy. *European Early Childhood Education Research Journal*, 24(1), 5–24.

Pascal, C., Bertram, T. and Rouse, L. (2019) *Getting it Right in the Early Years Foundation Stage: A Review, Early Education*. Available at: www.early-education.org.uk/getting-it-right-early-years-foundation-stage-review-evidence [Accessed 6 January 2024].

Payler, J., Wood, E., Georgeson, J., Davis, G., Jarvis, P., Rose, J., Gilbert, L., Hood, P., Mitchell, H. and Chesworth, L. (2017) *BERA-TACTYC Early Childhood Research Review 2003–2017*. Available at: http://oro.open.ac.uk/50282/ [Accessed 6 March 2024].

Shore, R. (2003) *Rethinking the Brain: New Insights into Early Development*. New York: Families and Work Institute.

7

LITERACY

> *I have defined early reading as heterogeneous – providing opportunities for under-threes to be immersed in the concept of language, stories, storytelling; accessing and 'sharing' stories, reading images, accessing paper, print and screen texts, experimenting with language patterns, rhyme, rhythm and beat.*
>
> Boardman, 2019, p. 116

INTRODUCTION

Ask any parent what they expect their child will learn to do in the first few years of school and 'learning to read and write' is highly likely to be one of the first things they talk about. The way that reading has been taught in schools has been the subject of much discussion throughout my own teaching career, although phonics has always been a part of the process.

In 1998, as literacy lead in a very small school, Ruth was sent on National Literacy Strategy training – a highly prescriptive approach which dictated that literacy should be taught for an hour a day from Reception onwards; it even included a clock to tell us what we should be teaching and when. The strategy promoted a searchlights approach to reading and although phonics was part of this strategy there was a focus on Onset and Rime and good sight word knowledge.

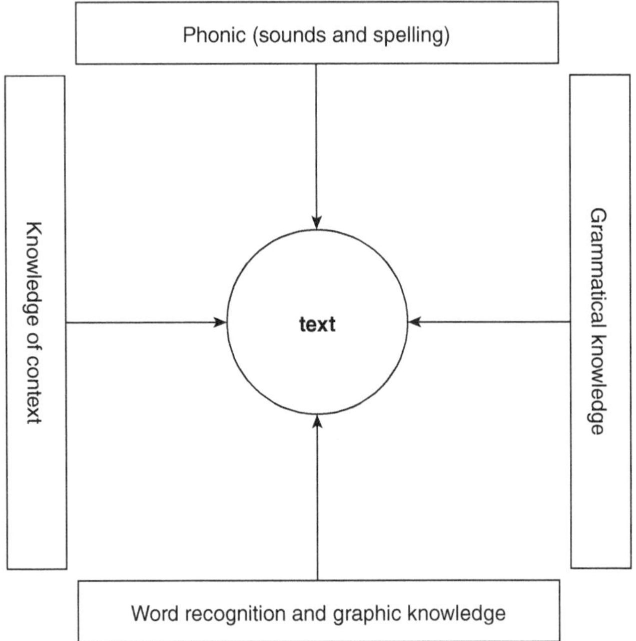

Figure 7.1 Searchlights model from the National Literacy Strategy

In 1999, the government released *Progression in Phonics* (DfE, 1999) after meeting with Dianne McGuinness, who was critical of the searchlights model. There was more emphasis on the analysis of spoken words into phonemes, but the focus on grapheme–phoneme correspondences were taught at a much slower pace than we would in the classroom today. This was followed, in 2004, by *Playing with Sounds* (DfES, 2004) specifically designed for Reception children.

In the meantime, momentum was building around the teaching of synthetic phonics; a longitudinal study was taking place in Scotland, carried out by Johnston and Watson (2005), on the impact of synthetic phonics on early reading. What became known as the 'Clackmannanshire report' would go on to influence the English approach to teaching young children to read. Following Jim Rose's review of the teaching of early reading in 2006, the government introduced *Letters and Sounds* for all schools to follow (DfES, 2007). The national expectations that every school in England would provide synthetic phonics teaching for at least 20 minutes every day in Reception and Key Stage 1 and that the 44 phonemes would be taught by the end of the autumn term in Reception were established. In 2010, the Phonics Screening Check (PSC) was introduced (DfE, 2010) and would later become much more than a screening check, with schools having inspections triggered by low PSC results. The 'reading wars' were discussed regularly and hotly debated on social media and in the press.

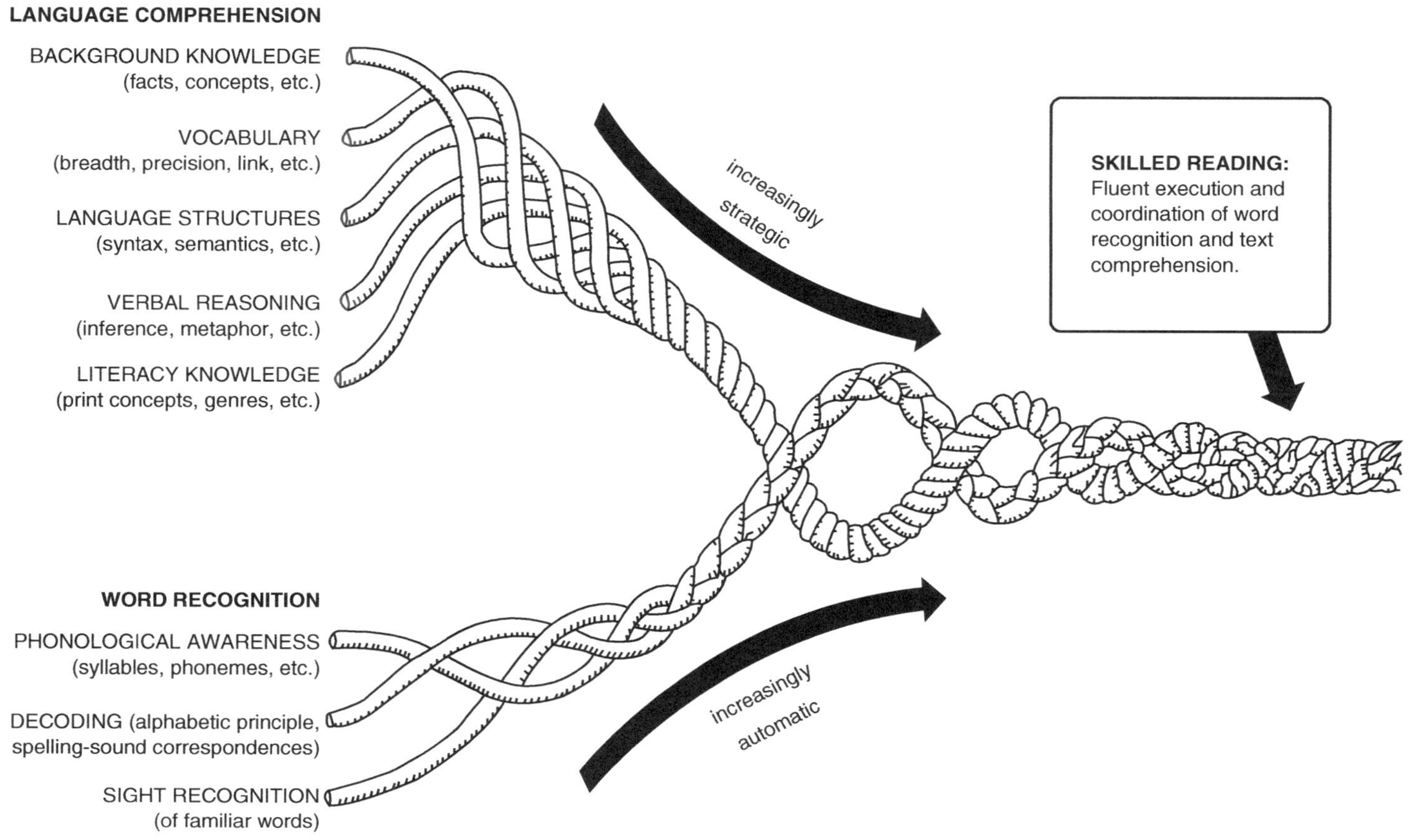

Figure 7.2 Reading rope

Source: Scarborough, 2001, p. 25.

It is fair to say that phonics has dominated the teaching of reading throughout my career, and I have had excellent results teaching hundreds of children to decode using phonics. I am a fan! But I also recognise that phonics is a tool in the literacy tool kit, and does not equate to reading or writing. Having secure phonic knowledge and skills will support children to become effective readers and writers; it is much harder for children to carry out these tasks when they don't have secure phonic knowledge. But phonic knowledge alone is not enough.

Dr Hollis Scarborough identified the many different skills and 'strands' children need to be skilled readers, when she developed her *reading rope* model (2001) (see Figure 7.2 on page 83).

Phonics is a vital strand in the rope. It is important but it will not support children with their comprehension. Other factors are also important.

This aligns with the recent changes to the *understanding the world* educational programme, which acknowledges the impact of children's experiences and knowledge of the world on their ability to read for meaning.

> As well as building important knowledge, this extends their familiarity with words that support understanding across domains. Enriching and widening children's vocabulary will support later reading comprehension.
>
> (DfE, 2024)

WHERE ARE WE NOW?

In April 2021, the DfE announced that they would be launching a new validation programme for phonics schemes, and that Letters and Sounds would no longer meet the criteria to achieve this validation.

The DfE gave the following reasons for these changes:

> The way in which phonics is taught in schools has evolved significantly in the last 10 years. The 2007 Letters and Sounds handbook isn't a full Systematic Synthetic Phonics (SSP) programme because it doesn't provide the support, guidance, resources or training needed. It relies on schools building a programme of resources around the handbook and in many cases updating the progression to bring it in line with current best practice.
>
> (DfE, 2021)

What followed, while schools were still in the middle of the pandemic and dealing with lockdowns, was, for many, a rush to purchase a validated scheme if they weren't already using one. Given that this announcement was made after the school budget had been set for the year ahead, this proved highly problematic, particularly for small schools who didn't have the staffing resources to investigate all the validated schemes in depth, or the money to purchase some of the resources required.

The impact of this policy, coupled with Ofsted's focus on early reading, has led to some developmentally inappropriate practice for our youngest children – at a time when they have already missed out on some of the important early skills of socialising, communicating and moving.

The focus on 'fidelity' to schemes written for 'broadly typical' children, pre-pandemic, has meant that some children spend a lot of time 'keeping up' with additional phonics sessions which take the staff away from the provision and children away from play and other areas of learning.

In some settings, reading and phonics now account for over 50 per cent of the timetable for children who have been identified as 'falling behind', regardless of their month of birth. All children are expected to keep up with the programme. The issue here is that, 'there is no evidence to support giving mathematics and literacy greater emphasis than any other areas of learning within the EYFS' (Pascal et al., 2019, p. 8). In fact, prioritising higher-order literacy skills before a child has secure development in oral language could lead to problems for children (Dockrell et al., 2010; Payler et al., 2017). Levy (2009) advises that staged reading systems should be used cautiously, and that children should be actively encouraged to explore a range of reading skills and texts.

Very few people would argue that phonics isn't a useful tool in the literacy tool kit, but its current dominance of the Reception landscape is not necessarily conducive to children's overall development and the development of a lifelong love of reading, which the DfE outlines in the Literacy Educational Programme.

THE RIGHT THINGS AT THE RIGHT TIME

A perhaps unintended consequence of the current focus on phonics is that some of the necessary pre-phonic skills are sometimes overlooked as the push from Ofsted to start with grapheme–phoneme correspondences (GPCs) impacts on teachers' priorities. Phase one of the Letters and Sounds programme has been dismissed by some as a 'waste of time', but children need to develop a range of pre-phonic skills if they are to be able to successfully blend and segment and discriminate sounds. This has led to some Reception classes no longer focusing on these areas and even some nurseries and preschools introducing formal GPC teaching before children start school, although Ofsted and the DfE have made it quite clear that this is not an expectation.

In fact, this could be highly detrimental for some children. Derbyshire et al. (2014) identify that decontextualised teaching, which is unsympathetic of children's experiences, can be inaccessible and can undermine the unique abilities of the child. By starting with phonics too early we could put children off reading. Of course, there are exceptions, and it's important to focus on the unique child and their needs. There may well be some children who are ready to access GPCs before they start Reception, but there are key skills that should be in place before we rush to do this because we perceive it is what is expected of us.

It would be undesirable to argue that we should not teach phonics systematically to children when they are ready, so that they can work on the other skills of reading and writing and develop a lifelong love of literacy. In this chapter we will explore what other aspects of early literacy we need to develop in our youngest children, so that we can encourage them to be lifelong readers and writers.

SECURING FIRM FOUNDATIONS

The move towards more formal GPC teaching in nurseries should be considered carefully by practitioners; just because we can do something, it doesn't mean it will be beneficial to children. We only have a certain amount of time with the children and we need to ensure that prime areas are secure. Communication and language and physical development are essential prerequisites for becoming a reader and writer. Despite the DfE being quite clear that there is no expectation to do this, I have even been asked about phonics teaching for two-year-olds. Of course, there are things that we can do to support children to develop their early phonological awareness so that they have a sound foundation for phonics teaching later on, but this does not mean that we should replicate what happens in Reception.

There are numerous studies (Dockrell, 2010; Payler et al., 2017) that show that children who have a securely developed understanding of spoken language, vocabulary and strong comprehension skills are better placed to acquire the necessary skills to decode and develop as a reader. All of these skills can be developed in a language- and literacy-rich environment.

WHAT DOES A LITERACY-RICH ENVIRONMENT LOOK LIKE?

People often mistake a literacy-rich environment for one which is covered in print. But this can be problematic. If we are teaching children that the most efficient way to learn to read is to decode words phonetically, putting random words on the wall out of context, many of which are not phonetically decodable, is not really reinforcing this message. Contextualised words can be helpful – for example, labels for resources, or to help children know where to store things. But we should use these labels judiciously, otherwise they can be overwhelming, or they can also feel like 'wallpaper' and lack purpose. Careful thought should be given to what we label and how.

A language- and literacy-rich environment provides children with opportunities to talk, to share, to listen, to hold 'serve and return' conversations with adults and their peers (see Chapter 4) and where singing, stories, rhymes and poetry are an integral part of daily routines.

Books are selected carefully to encourage children to develop a love of reading. Careful thought is given to linking texts to children's interests, the topics being taught in the curriculum and to exposing children to well-loved stories and rhymes.

A literacy-rich environment encourages children to read for pleasure; the book area should be cosy and inviting, books should be displayed so that children can see their covers where possible, in order to entice them to read. Children who don't see themselves as readers should have something which draws them into the book area. In some classes I have used puppets to help children retell familiar stories, story sacks with objects from the stories to encourage children to see reading as something which is enjoyable, collections of well-loved stories that the children know well so that they can enjoy familiar texts. The books should be 'the star of the show' in the reading area; our aim is to draw children in to the space so that they can focus on reading. It is important not to overwhelm children, so choose books wisely and don't have too many.

Stories should be shared with the whole group every day and adults should make time to read with children when they are in the provision, if the children are keen to read.

Literacy-rich environments provide a range of mark-making tools throughout the provision and different types of paper, books, envelopes, booklets and leaflets, whiteboards, markers, chalkboards, chalks and pens to encourage children to write wherever they are. Toolboxes and caddies placed indoors and out provide a range of writing opportunities and writing and mark-making opportunities are valued throughout the setting.

Outdoors provides opportunities for children to develop the necessary prerequisite physical skills for developing as readers and writers (see Chapter 6 for further details). There should be plenty of opportunities to develop proprioception, core, shoulder and upper-body strength, as well as opportunities to mark-make in different ways. Outdoors should be larger, louder and more physically challenging. Providing whiteboards and chalkboards on walls and fences helps children to develop their shoulder girdles by making large arching movements; whiteboards and markers give different feedback to the children. For children in the early stages of writing or who have less strength in their arms, whiteboards are an easy way to make marks as the marker glides on the surface. A chalkboard requires greater strength as the chalkboard provides resistance against the chalk; the child will have to push harder to make the marks. This can be motivating and provide excellent feedback to the child in terms of proprioception, but might be challenging for children with weaker upper-body and shoulder-girdle strength. Opportunities to mark-make should not be restricted to writing. We should value and praise all the mark-making children do. Often children will draw and make visual representations; these should be given high status in the Early Years setting.

How educators '*respond* and *what they value* helps to form children's attitudes towards writing and determine the paths their learning journeys will follow' (Mackenzie, 2014, p. 189, emphasis added).

THE MYTH ABOUT WHITEBOARDS AND MARKERS

In the reading framework published in 2021 (which has been critiqued by some experts in early literacy) and reissued in 2023 the DfE states:

> Sitting on the floor and writing on a mini whiteboard does not help children learn to hold a pencil and form letters correctly. To write, they should sit comfortably on a chair at a table. Using a whiteboard also means there is no paper record of the work, for the child, the teacher, or the parent.
>
> (DfE, 2023)

There is no research evidence to support the view that using whiteboards and markers doesn't help children to hold a pencil and form letters correctly. In fact, the use of larger writing materials is a widely recognised step towards holding a pencil later. For the child whose hands are still quite chubby in the early stages of writing, a marker pen can provide a useful bridge to a pencil. Writing with a pencil also requires a significant amount of strength in the arm to put the right amount of pressure on the page. Most practitioners will be familiar with the spindly, 'spideresque' writing that children who have not developed this strength produce. Whiteboards and markers give excellent feedback to reluctant writers, the marker glides smoothly on the surface giving the child instant feedback and a sense of success. Of course, the aim is to move towards writing with a pencil when the child is ready, but we don't have to miss out stages which can help the children to get there, just because the DfE don't like whiteboards and markers.

I am not sure why there is such concern about keeping a paper record of everything the child does in the classroom. If the child was only writing in the phonics lessons, then of course it would be important to keep a record of significant moments where the child achieves and these can always be recorded by photocopying particularly significant pieces of work if they're written on a whiteboard. But the children are writing every day, across a range of contexts; staff will have a range of recorded 'evidence' and the DfE itself has stated several times in the EYFS profile handbook: 'Sources of written or photographic evidence are not required and teachers should not record evidence' (DfE, 2023). It seems bizarre that the reading framework appears to put such an emphasis on this, as it runs counter to DfE advice elsewhere.

When we are teaching children to write we need them to be able to sit comfortably and if we're focusing on letter formation and handwriting sitting at a table will help with this, providing we have the correct-height chairs and tables. But writing takes many forms in the classroom and is not always formal. Sometimes we want children to write things at speed and for the youngest children we want them to see writing as communication, to share their thoughts and feelings and to be enthusiastic about doing so. Insisting that all writing should take place at a table, with pencils and paper or books may not be conducive to this. The framework doesn't actually say that all writing must take place at a table or with pencils, but this is the way that some people (including some inspectors) have interpreted this comment. One nursery I worked with had removed all mark-making equipment other than pencils and paper as a result of this statement. The impact was that some children who had previously been enthused mark-makers and were writing for pleasure ceased to do so. I'm not sure that was quite the result they were hoping for.

As with every piece of advice, unless it's in the Statutory Framework, practitioners need to look at it through their own unique lens. We want to get children writing and to enjoy mark-making and communicating with others. If whiteboards and markers provide an opportunity to start the journey and children find them helpful, then practitioners should think about using them, and providing a range of other mark-making tools and materials. They should also provide opportunities for children to develop their writing skills at tables with support from adults. The two approaches are not mutually exclusive. There is much debate currently about writing in Early Years, with a push from certain phonics schemes to approach this purely through dictation. Dictation has a place and is certainly helpful for supporting children's phonic knowledge and developing their secretarial skills.

We must always remember that the purpose of writing is to communicate and the desire to communicate starts in infancy. Young children who see adults writing will naturally want to copy them. They will want to record and share their thoughts and we should encourage them to do so wherever possible by providing a range of materials and resources in our continuous provision, by providing support and encouragement to do so, and by celebrating their successes. Writing is hard work. When we look at the skills necessary to be a successful writer, it is hardly surprising that many children find the task tricky (see Figure 7.3).

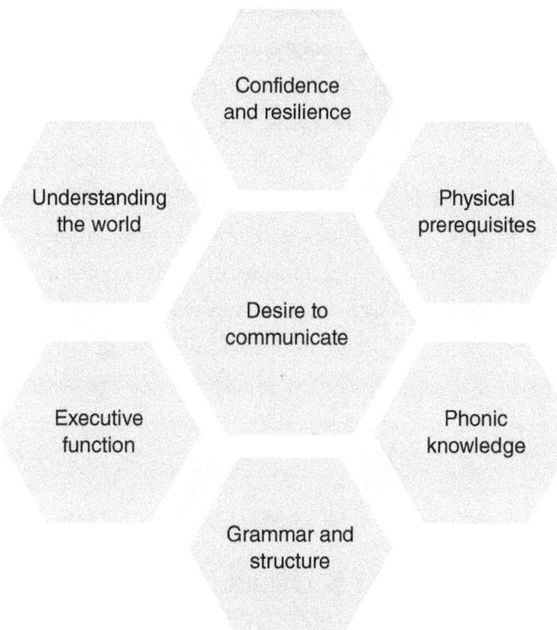

Figure 7.3 Writing matrix

Source: Swailes, 2023.

BEFORE WE GET TO RECEPTION

Much of this chapter has reflected on the current debates about the teaching of literacy in schools and how they have impacted on practice in Early Years, most notably in Reception. As with all government policy, what affects primary practice today inevitably moves into Early Years and there is an increasing pressure on practitioners working with the youngest children to ensure they are ready to read. Reading is an important skill; many of the physical prerequisites for literacy have been covered in our earlier chapter on physical development. What other aspects must we consider if we are to secure the foundations of early literacy? The term 'emergent literacy' describes the skills, knowledge and understanding children acquire prior to formal literacy learning (Edwards, 2014). As practitioners we can ensure that we provide opportunities to develop these key skills.

Young children need to see adults reading and writing, to know that print carries meaning, to know that English is read from left to right and from top to bottom by tracking. They need to know how to hold a book, turn the pages of a book and look after a book properly. They should enjoy stories, rhymes, songs, poems as part of their everyday offer in the setting. Adults should point out text to the children and young children will often learn words which are meaningful to them. My elder daughter 'read' the label on the Marmite® jar at 18 months; of course, she wasn't really reading, but the typeface and the jar were familiar to her and we regularly named objects as we were chatting to her. Oral language plays a significant role in children's emergent literacy (Chapter 4 on language and communication should be read in conjunction with this chapter). Young children will tune into the prosody of speech and the intonation in words, identifying sounds and syllables and developing their auditory discrimination by being exposed to a range of different sounds and experiences. Visual processing skills are vital for literacy and all these core concepts are assimilated and developed through multiple daily interactions and experiences. In the home, Shea (2011) refers to the teaching of emergent literacy as 'soft teaching', where children are supported by responsive adults who answer their questions and spark further curiosity. The impact of these early experiences has been widely documented and there is evidence to support the idea that a lack of these early experiences makes becoming literate more challenging (Clay, 1991; Hartas, 2011). With this in mind, we need to ensure that we provide a wealth of experiences for children, from those early interactions and discussions to sharing texts, meaningful labels, playing alongside and modelling language and communication, singing songs, playing with sounds and engaging in soft teaching to support children to be successful, literate adults.

REFLECTION 7.1

Consider the age and stage of the children you're working with; what soft teaching do you need to put in place to ensure the foundations are secure for later literacy?

Do your children see you as a reader and a writer?

How do you choose the books and rhymes you share with your children?

Are there ways you could incorporate more singing and rhymes into your daily routines?

KEY POINTS OF THE CHAPTER

There are extensive research studies into the teaching of early reading, and it is a widely contested area of discussion.

The emphasis on synthetic phonics has impacted on the way that reading is taught in the Early Years and has become more tightly controlled over the last few years.

Phonics is an important tool in the reading toolkit and helps children to access a range of resources, we must also develop children's comprehension skills and their love of reading.

Literacy is linked to many other areas of learning, including communication and language, understanding the world, expressive arts and design, personal social and emotional development and physical development.

REFERENCES

Boardman, K. (2019) Too young to read: Early Years practitioners' perceptions of early reading with under-threes. *International Journal of Early Years Education*, 20(2), 114–129.

Clay, M. (1991) *Becoming Literate: The Construction of Inner Control*. Portsmouth, NH: Heinemann.

Department for Education (DfE) (1999) *Progression in Phonics: Materials for Whole-class Teaching*. Available at: https://dera.ioe.ac.uk/id/eprint/4419/1/CDtext.pdf [Accessed 29 May 2024].

DfE (2010) *Primary Framework for Literacy and Mathematics*. Available at: https://webarchive.nationalarchives.gov.uk/ukgwa/20100603153934/http://nationalstrategies.standards.dcsf.gov.uk/primary/primaryframework/literacyframework [Accessed 10 April 2024].

DfE (2021) *DfE Validation of Systematic Synthetic Phonics (SSP) Programmes*. Available at: https://view.officeapps.live.com/op/view.aspx?src=https%3A%2F%2Fassets.publishing.service.gov.uk%2Fmedia%2F6065d0848fa8f515aa902c44%2FSelf_Assessment_Form_SSP.odt&wdOrigin=BROWSELINK [Accessed 21 March 2024].

DfE (2023) *The Reading Framework*. Available at: www.gov.uk/government/publications/the-reading-framework-teaching-the-foundations-of-literacy [Accessed 1 January 2024].

DfE (2024) *Early Years Foundation Stage (EYFS) Statutory Framework*. Available at: www.gov.uk/government/publications/early-years-foundation-stage-framework--2 [Accessed 1 January 2024].

Department for Education and Skills (DfES) (2004) *Playing with Sounds: A Supplement to Progression in Phonics*. London: DfES.

DfES (2007) *Letters and Sounds: Principles and Practice of High Quality Phonics*. Available at: https://assets.publishing.service.gov.uk/media/5a7aa7b6e5274a34770e630c/Letters_and_Sounds_-_DFES-00281-2007.pdf [Accessed 29 May 2024].

Derbyshire, N., Finn, B., Griggs, S. and Ford, C. (2014) An unsure start for young children in English urban primary schools. *Urban Review*, 46(5), 816–830.

Dockrell, J.E., Stuart, M. and King, D. (2010) Supporting early oral language skills for English language learners in inner city preschool provision. *British Journal of Educational Psychology*, 80(4), 497–515.

Edwards, C.M. (2014) Maternal literacy practices and toddlers' emergent literacy skills. *Journal of Early Childhood Literacy*, 14, 53–79.

Hartas, D. (2011) Families' social backgrounds matter: Socio-economic factors, home learning and young children's language, literacy and social outcomes. *British Educational Research Journal*, 37(6), 893–914.

Johnston, R. and Watson, J. (2005) *The Effects of Synthetic Phonics Teaching on Reading and Spelling Attainment: A Seven Year Longitudinal Study*. Available at: https://dera.ioe.ac.uk/id/eprint/14793/1/0023582.pdf [Accessed 1 April 2024].

Levy, R. (2009) Children's perceptions of reading and the use of reading scheme texts. *Cambridge Journal of Education*, 39(3), 361–377.

Mackenzie, N. (2014) Teaching early writers: Teachers' responses to a young child's writing sample. *Australian Journal of Language and Literacy*, 37(3), 182–191.

Pascal, C., Bertram, T. and Rouse, L. (2019) *Getting it Right in the Early Years Foundation Stage: A Review*. Early Education. Available at: www.early-education.org.uk/getting-it-right-early-years-foundation-stage-review-evidence [Accessed 7 January 2024].

Payler, J., Georgeson, J. and Barber, J. (2017) The professional development needs of Early Years practitioners: Evidence from the Effective Provision of Preschool Education (EPPE) project. *Journal of Early Childhood Research*, 15(1), 5–24.

Scarborough, H. (2001) Connecting early language and literacy to later reading (dis)abilities: Evidence, theory, and practice. In S.B. Neuman and D.K. Dickinson, *Handbook of Early Literacy Research* (pp. 97–110). New York: Guilford.

Shea, T.M. (2011) Home learning environments: A case study of family literacy practices and change in a low-income home. *Urban Education*, 46(5), 984–1008.

Swailes, R. (2023) Broad and balanced? A look at the impact of approved phonic schemes on the Curriculum. *Early Years Educator*, 23(20), 29–33.

8

MATHEMATICS

> *Mathematics could be like roller-skating, but usually it is like being told stop roller-skating and come in and tidy your room.*
>
> *This is not a superficial matter.*
>
> Winter, 1992, p. 99

INTRODUCTION

Children's development of mathematics begins at an early age. Mathematical experiences early in life provide a foundation for future development. Maths is introduced to babies through their senses in the first few months of their lives: contrasting colours, tactile objects and toys banging on the floor are all stimuli to their developing brains. According to recent research, even babies under one year of age have a keen sense of numbers and quantities. These babies can clearly distinguish between sets of one, two and three objects. Evangelou's study (2009) found that young children often use their bodies to gain a deeper understanding of mathematical concepts such as time, space, direction and positioning.

Children's learning and development in mathematics are influenced by a variety of social factors as well as interactive practices. Research has shown that providing children with practical, purposeful experiences supports mathematic learning more effectively than doing the same activity without any specific goal (Gelman and Kalish, 2006). Studies have shown that children who are supported early in their mathematics development, especially at home, can achieve higher levels in mathematics and other areas of learning and development in the long term. Williams argues that the idea that babies and very young children are blank slates has been completely debunked by research over the last 30 years. In her book *Playful Mathematics for Children 3 to 7* (2022), she allows us to explore the notion that babies are irrational, amoral, unable to understand relationships between cause and effect (Gopnick et al., 2015).

WHERE DO WE START WITH MATHEMATICS?

There is an element of anxiety when it comes to mathematics. Because of our own educational experiences as children, it is very common for early childhood professionals to have negative feelings and a lack of confidence about mathematics. Williams (2022) explains that mathematics education has a poor track record for inspiring joy, creativity and love among the general public. When expressing their feelings about mathematics, early childhood professionals should be aware of their own internal biases. Children's enthusiasm for mathematics can be developed by everyone in the Early Years, and the most enjoyable way of doing this is through play.

MATHEMATICS IN SOCIETY

In every corner of the globe, mathematics can be found. Through shapes and patterns, the natural world provides excellent opportunities for children to explore mathematics. Do you ever take advantage of these opportunities when you are with children and assist them in discovering patterns and shapes through the objects around them? Every day, from waking up to going to bed, we are constantly exposed to mathematics. Numbers, dials, alarm clocks beeping in the morning, travelling through public transportation and in the car, walking and so on are all familiar to children. As a result of these daily activities, children are able to develop mathematics continuously.

DEVELOPING MATHEMATICS

Numerous theorists have argued that the approach to mathematical concepts is coordinated through children's play. Tucker (2014) and Haylock and Cockburn (2008) are among these theorists. According to them, children learn mathematics best through practical, meaningful experiences that are both purposeful and child-centred. In the Early Years, it is best to approach mathematics with joy, enthusiasm and abilities. It is believed that the more practical applications and activities children are exposed to, the more opportunities they will have to develop their mathematical skills on a daily basis.

Scholars believe that the key to children learning through play is having knowledgeable and skilled professionals provide high-quality experiences for them where they can extend their thinking and build on what they already know. The work of Piaget has had a significant impact on the field of education. A more child-initiated approach to learning has been developed as a result of his work. According to Piaget, children learn better if they are actively involved with their environment, including how they develop cognitively, as well as having access to a variety of materials provided by their teacher. As we move forward into the 21st century, we are becoming increasingly aware that children bring with them a wide range of knowledge when it comes to mathematical concepts and experiences. The development of mathematical skills begins as soon as a child is able to sit up. A child's understanding of quantity, their ability to compare shapes and sizes, and their use of early mathematical concepts is demonstrated while they play and engage in other aspects of their daily lives (Gopnik et al, 2001).

WHAT IS EARLY MATHEMATICS?

Mathematical concepts from the Early Years include counting, quantity, shapes, spatial awareness, measurement and patterns. Through the child's interaction with their environment, children develop a natural curiosity that facilitates exploration of concepts. In your early childhood settings, you can observe this when children explore mathematics while playing with blocks and building towers. By doing this, children notice shapes and colours, and they begin to categorise the shapes based on their size.

All aspects of mathematics education require high-quality research grounded in theory in order to progress and contribute to the generation of new knowledge from which the educational practice can benefit. Due to the evidence that later mathematics development is laid in the Early Years (e.g., Duncan et al., 2007; Krajewski and Schneider 2009; Levine et al., 2011), such high-quality research is of particular importance to early childhood mathematics education. The importance of early childhood mathematics for children's educational success has been recognised by both Gasteiger and Benz (2018) and Cross et al. (2009). Gasteiger and Benz (2018) state: 'Early childhood mathematics education played little role for many years, but today it is clearly imperative to pay attention to children's early mathematics development' (p. 109).

It is important to maintain a child-centred approach and develop the importance of play when it comes to mathematical development. Teachers also have an important role to play in making sure that play pedagogy is at the centre of mathematical teaching. The ELGs, which describe what children should be expected to accomplish at the end of the academic year, provide little guidance regarding what children should actually learn. Children's depth of knowledge has recently been emphasised in the ELGs in relation to the recognition and understanding of numbers, number relations, quantity and patterns (DfE, 2021). According to Gilmore et al. (2018), domain-specific number skills play a critical role in the development of later mathematical abilities, including the ability to recognise quantities of up to four or five items without counting and understand the composition of numbers up to ten.

PLAY AND MATHEMATICAL DEVELOPMENT

A recent systematic review concluded that *guided play*, also known as *play-based learning*, was more effective than direct instruction and free play in improving children's early numerical skills and shape knowledge (Skene et al., 2022). In early childhood education and in a child's daily life, play has a significant role to work for a child's development. Mathematical concepts are sometimes directly addressed in the child's play. As a result of this process, a child's mathematical development is supported and they are inspired to think logically about mathematics. Mathematics play has a relatively short history, with roots going back to pioneers such as Montessori, who explained children's concepts of mathematics. In order to strengthen mathematical concepts and skills in young learners, it is important to add materials to sustain interest or generate new learning.

RESOURCES TO SUPPORT YOUR MATHS PLAY AREAS

- An interactive counting library featuring a variety of containers, things to count and labels to write
- An instrument for weighing
- Tools for measuring
- Construction
- Number lines
- Maths picture and story books

We are now going to give you some ideas on how you can introduce certain resources for different mathematical concepts; for example, subitising, numbers and counting and block and shape play. We see Early Years provisions focus on maths areas. Even though this can be inviting, this is not always necessary. Your Early Years provision should incorporate mathematical opportunities where children can explore maths through everyday play.

When thinking about maths areas in your Early Years provision, consider some reflective opportunities for your practice.

- Are the resources provided in a manner that allows children to lay them out, manipulate them and explore them?

- Do the resources provide a variety of options, are they appealing to children and are they open-ended?
- Is there a resource that supports number, pattern and spatial reasoning within mathematics?
- Does the resource support a 'hands-on', practical approach to mathematics (including games and manipulatives for the child to handle)?
- Can resources be easily accessed and returned?
- Does the resource have the potential to be used in a variety of ways in the future?

SUBITISING

Subitising refers to the ability to recognise the number of objects in a small group without having to count them, a concept devised by the theorist Piaget. Often, this is explained by referring to a dice – we can instantly identify the number of dots without having to count each one separately.

Early childhood maths curriculum is primarily focused on developing an understanding of numbers, as any early childhood educator knows. Children need to be able to relate numbers to actual objects or groups of objects in order to develop a sense of number in the Early Years. Number conservation refers to this process. Children often learn how to count by rote without fully understanding the meaning behind their actions. Children can begin to understand how numbers are composed by observing groups of items.

Young children particularly enjoy manipulating objects physically. It is possible for teachers to develop a variety of engaging and fun subitising activities to engage children in mathematics (see examples below).

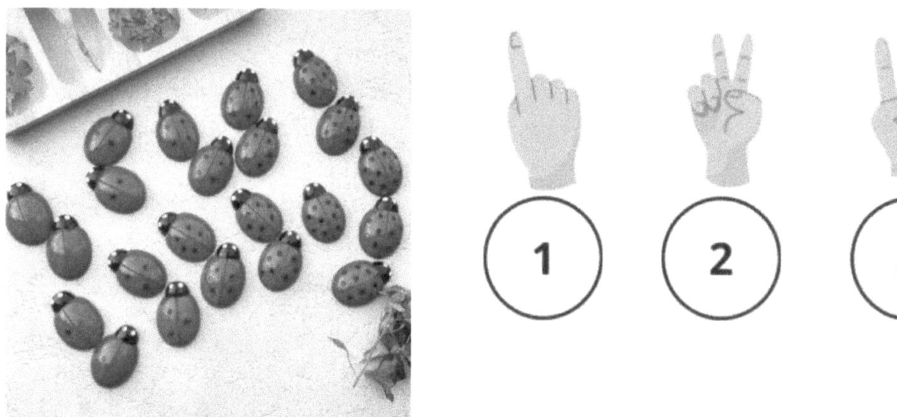

Figure 8.1 Examples of subitising activities

Note: Ladybird photo courtesy Oak and Ever.

REFLECTION 8.1

Children's development and understanding can be assessed by early childhood professionals by asking them questions such as:

- do you see a number of dots?
- can you tell me how many dots there are?
- I can see that you have grouped them differently; why is that?
- can you tell me how many dots you need to make?

It would be beneficial to use natural resources as well as number cards and objects that can be sorted in order to promote number sense in children and to provide them with a range of games and activities that will engage them in mathematics.

NUMBERS

Early development requires an understanding of numbers and the ability to recognise them. At the age of three, children are capable of recognising many numbers and learning how to compare large and small objects. As children grow, they begin to understand the numbers and how they are arranged within them, for example, the number 4 is greater than the number 1. Children who learn number recognition early will develop their maths confidence, develop their critical thinking skills and establish a foundation for success in mathematics.

It is common for two-year-old children to be able to count to ten even if their numbers are mixed up. Building a strong foundation for number fluency begins with practising numbers and counting. Counting numbers daily and playing fun games can make learning fun for children. Even rhymes and stories can be used to count. Children can learn and recognise numbers in a fun and enjoyable manner through books such as *The Very Hungry Caterpillar* or *Farm 123*.

CASE STUDY 8.1

ERICA, NURSERY PRACTITIONER: TWO-YEAR-OLDS' ROOM

In order to help her two-year-old children develop their mathematical skills, Erica has started thinking about what they need. Although Helen Williams' book *Playful Mathematics* (2022) is primarily for children three to seven years old, Erica finds that this book helps her understand what she can do with her children to help them develop further. In her explanation, Erica described how she does not expect her children to participate in mathematical adult-led activities, but that she ensures that there are plenty of opportunities within the provision to develop mathematical skills. Afterwards, Erica explores a number of things that she has developed in her room, including:

1. on the wall, there are shadows of numbers that the children must match. It's nothing special, but they're Velcro® and the children take out the numbers from the box and attach them to the shadow. Also, I have used switches that stick above the numbers, so when the children press them, they say number 1, number 2, etc.;
2. every week, we look at a certain number and try to incorporate it into the classroom's resources. Children are asked to go into the home corner and count two spoons, two dolls, etc. As they love interacting with us, the children love it as well;
3. every day, we sing nursery rhymes. There is always a flying saucer song, a little duck song and cards with numbers on them. The children are also encouraged to point to the numbers. While it can be slow at times, allowing children some time to think is a good thing to do. Other children usually tell or shout out the number if they have waited too long. All of it is part of the fun;
4. children can also use blocks and develop their mathematical awareness in our maths areas. The joy of seeing a child come to you with two blocks after playing and getting excited for us is so rewarding. Our programme must be child-led, and we love interacting with the children.

REFLECTION 8.2

- What do you do in your provision to develop mathematical development?
- Do you provide opportunities for children to develop mathematical skills in their own time and pace? If so, how do you do this? Think of some examples.
- Are you confident with providing mathematical activities and opportunities for children?
- Think about areas within your provision; do they give opportunities for mathematical development? For example, measuring cylinders, block play, counting stones, etc.

BLOCK AND SHAPE PLAY

In any early childhood classroom or setting, you will most definitely find blocks. The blocks, no matter how large or small, can help us develop our Early Years mathematical pedagogies. In addition to providing young children with entertainment, blocks offer a variety of benefits. Children's social, cognitive and physical development are nurtured through block play, contributing to a variety of learning experiences.

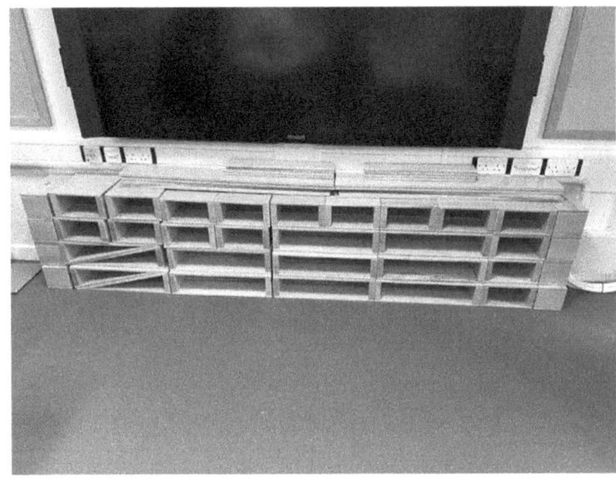

Figure 8.2 Blocks in an early childhood setting

A key benefit of block play is its ability to foster logical thinking. When children work with blocks, they learn how to solve problems, make patterns and represent the world around them. Blocks can be used to create symmetrical patterns to help children learn about balance and symmetry.

The play of unit blocks that relate to size and shape helps children integrate all the key spatial aspects they need to develop (Williams, 2022), such as:

- understanding the relationship between shapes, sizes, and parts and wholes;
- visualisation and memory development;
- language expansion;
- positioning and orienting oneself;
- rotation and transformation are two related concepts.

Williams (2022) argues that unit blocks are related, so two cubes will have the same volume. In addition to being based on a unit system, pattern blocks can be used to explore patterns in mathematics. Besides developing spatial reasoning, blocks also help children learn their numbers. There is an overlap between spatial and numerical reasoning. According to research, spatial reasoning is indicative of much later mathematical development (Cheng and Mix, 2014).

When children play with blocks, they practise mathematical skills. In Hirsch (1996), variable size and shape blocks are selected and compared to determine classification and separation. Children learn to visualise relationships when they play with blocks, since they measure lengths, widths, and heights (even with their eyes). Similar manipulatives will be used in later school years when studying shape, space and measure. It provides a lifetime of fun as well as valuable educational lessons. The names of geometric shapes, mathematical concepts that children will use to play with blocks and development stages exhibited by children during play would be beneficial knowledge for people who work with small children. Children should have access to unit blocks from an early age.

CASE STUDY 8.2: WRITTEN BY CURTIS MEIER (COMMUNITY PLAYTHINGS UK)

MATHS AND BLOCKS IN EARLY YEARS

Ian is recreating, in detail, a map of his favourite storybook village. His four-year-old coordination doesn't allow him to draw this map with pencil and paper, but with blocks he is amazingly adept. If he did not have this means by which to express his ideas, adults would have no way of knowing that Ian has an entire map memorised in his mind. He attempts to build a bridge but can't figure out how to get the blocks to balance. His teacher holds the key to a breakthrough solution, but it's early days, so she observes but offers no support. Ian eventually moves to other activities, but the challenge works in his mind overnight because the following morning, he quickly places the blocks and begins building bridges all over the room. He has cracked the problem and made the learning his own.

KEY TAKEAWAYS

1. Children can demonstrate mathematical concepts through blocks long before they can speak or write about them.
2. It's usually best to stand back and let children solve their problems with minimal adult intervention. This approach enables children to find their own solutions.

Initially, mathematical thinking develops as children experiment with the size, shape and weight of the blocks, experiencing forces and the effects of gravity.

(Continued)

When they first encounter blocks in the construction area, babies play with them as individual pieces. Eventually, a child will begin to stack, and then create. Gura writes, 'Repetition appears to be an important feature of materials mastery. As each block form is discovered, there is much refining and variation within the familiar. A particular block form may be constructed so often that the procedure becomes effortless' (1992, p. 10).

As the rules of physics are internalised, they master concepts of stability, proportion, design and symmetry. They are also experiencing first hand concepts such as volume, area, distance and even addition and subtraction as they add or remove blocks.

THE SCIENCE OF BLOCK PLAY, MATHS AND SHAPES

Many early childhood experts, including Friedrich Froebel, Caroline Pratt, Harriet Johnson, Elizabeth Hirsch and Mary Jo Pollman (2010), have documented the value of blocks for children's learning, offering evidence that when children are given time to plan, construct and create with blocks, they develop socially, emotionally, cognitively and physically (Hansel, 2017, p. 5). This evidence is now being confirmed by scientists using new technologies to see the inner workings of the brain.

According to Dr Jo Boaler, a professor of mathematics education at Stanford University, brain research now shows that as you learn something deeply, the synaptic activity in the brain will create lasting connections (unlike when you learn something in a superficial way) and that 'synapses fire when we have conversations, play games, or build with toys' (Boaler, 2016, p. 1). In other words, building with blocks to experience their three-dimensional properties will create a lasting pathway in the brain and a deeper understanding of shape, whereas identifying three-dimensional shapes on a workbook page is unlikely to build understanding of shape and three-dimensionality.

THE IMPORTANCE OF SPATIAL SKILLS

In addition, there is exciting new evidence linking good spatial skills and children's future achievement in all the STEM (science, technology, engineering and mathematics) subjects (Lubinski, 2013; Newcombe, 2010). 'Despite the evidence, however, the importance of spatial skills is often overlooked as a key feature of STEM education. This frequent neglect of spatial development creates an additional barrier to children's STEM learning' (Berkowicz and Myers, 2017) and reminds those of us in early childhood education that we must start paying attention to developing spatial skills. While laying the foundation in the STEM subjects is important – especially for underserved populations and those underrepresented in the STEM fields, including girls – spatial skills are critical in many other fields, as well as in everyday life, such as when we load up a trunk with blocks and navigate our way to a new location for the first time.

The great news is that spatial skills can be improved with practice. While not all experts agree on a common definition of what spatial skills are (Hansel, 2017, p. 20), most agree that the use of manipulatives helps children make sense of abstract concepts. Wooden unit blocks are a perfect example of a child-friendly manipulative that can be used to strengthen spatial skills. Think about how a child recreates a zoo with blocks while closely referring to a map of the zoo and carefully ensuring that each zoo animal fits into the enclosures she has made to scale.

Which block activities foster spatial skills?

Start with giving children ample time for open-ended exploration with blocks, but don't stop there. If you really want to see children's spatial thinking flourish, target the spatial skills in and offer block activities that encourage spatial language and challenging tasks.

FAMILIES PLAY A PART IN MATHEMATICAL DEVELOPMENT

Developing children's mathematics and numeracy skills requires the involvement of their families. Similarly to educators, family members' attitudes and beliefs about mathematics and numeracy have a significant impact on children's engagement with and development of these skills. Families can provide opportunities to explore mathematics and provide support to children in becoming confident about mathematics and numeracy education since numeracy in the Early Years is so heavily woven into daily life.

Families can be encouraged by educators to take on a role in supporting children's mathematics and numeracy learning in a variety of ways. Informal conversations promote positive attitudes and reinforce responses that help children build their confidence, as well as formal communication with families (for example, in a family handbook or newsletter) about how they can support their children at home. Learning outcomes are more likely to improve when educators share ideas with families about children's mathematics and numeracy.

KEY POINTS OF THE CHAPTER

It is clear that mathematics has a large place within the structure of learning within the Early Years Foundation Stage. We should all be confident as Early Years professionals to deliver mathematics through the concept of play.

(Continued)

The chapter has explored the need to think about mathematics through everyday teaching opportunities. Play and continuous provision is key to teaching mathematics. Adult-led teaching also has its place to embed mathematical concepts.

It is important to note that educators' own beliefs and attitudes regarding mathematics and numeracy have a significant impact on how these ideas are incorporated into the learning environment for children. Several studies have identified that many early childhood educators have experienced negative mathematics experiences in their schooling (Anders and Rossbach, 2015) and therefore believe they cannot adequately support children in this area. For adults, it is crucial to take the time to reflect on their anxiety in relation to mathematics and to change their perception of the opportunities mathematics offers to make their lives more fulfilling. Early childhood educators have excellent numeracy skills and are competent users of mathematical concepts. Despite this, these skills are not always recognised as a positive and necessary aspect of their daily lives.

Focus on the key aspects of early mathematics below.

- In the Early Years environment, children can solve maths problems by using opportunities that arise throughout the day.
- Openly discuss how you use mathematics with children by doing this aloud and describing how you think and solve problems.
- Take advantage of interactions to develop children's understanding of mathematics: ask questions that stimulate and extend a child's knowledge and understanding of numbers, shapes and measures.
- Provide opportunities and resources that allow children to develop and extend their mathematical thinking in a variety of play situations, taking into consideration the interests and needs of the children.
- Provide parents with mathematical resources: lend picture books, games and other resources to support their children's mathematical development at home.

REFERENCES

Anders, Y. and Rossbach, H.-G. (2015) Preschool teachers' sensitivity to mathematics in children's play: The influence of math-related school experiences, emotional attitudes, and pedagogical beliefs. *Journal of Research in Childhood Education* (3), 305–322.

Berkowicz, J. and Myers, A. (2017) *Spatial Skills: A Neglected Dimension of Early STEM Education*. Available at: www.edweek.org/teaching-learning/opinion-spatial-skills-a-neglected-dimension-of-early-stem-education/2017/02 [Accessed 1 January 2024].

Boaler, J. (2016) *Mathematical Mindsets: Unleashing Students' Potential through Creative Math, Inspiring Messages and Innovative Teaching*. San Francisco, CA: Jossey-Bass.

Campbell, R. (2010) *Farm 123*. London: Macmillan.

Carle, E. (1969) *The Very Hungry Caterpillar*. London: Puffin.

Cheng, Y.-L. and Mix, K.S. (2014) Spatial training improves children's mathematics ability. *Journal of Cognition and Development*, 15(1), 2–11. https://doi.org/10.1080/15248372.2012.725186

Cross, C.T., Woods, T.A. and Schweingruber, H. (2009) *Mathematics Learning in Early Childhood: Paths Toward Excellence and Equity*. Washington, DC: National Academies Press.

Department for Education (DfE) (2021) *Early Years Foundation Stage Profile. EYFS Reforms Early Adopter Version*. Available at: https://assets.publishing.service.gov.uk/media/5f68b0eb8fa8f50763644e5e/Early_adopter_schools_EYFS_profile_handbook.pdf [Accessed 1 January 2024].

Duncan, G.J., Dowsett, C.J., Claessens, A., Magnuson, K., Huston, A.C., Klebanov, P., Pagani, L.S., Feinstein, L., Engel, M., Brooks-Gunn, J., Sexton, H., Duckworth, K. and Japel, C. (2007) School readiness and later achievement. *Developmental Psychology*, 43(6), 1428–1446.

Evangelou, M. (2009) *Early Years Learning and Development: Literature Review*. Available at: https://dera.ioe.ac.uk/id/eprint/11382/ [Accessed 1 January 2024].

Gasteiger, H. and Benz, C. (2018) Enhancing and analyzing kindergarten teachers' professional knowledge for early mathematics education. *Journal of Mathematical Behavior*, 51, 109–117. https://doi.org/10.1016/j.jmathb.2018.01.002

Gelman, S.A. and Kalish, C.W. (2006) Conceptual development. In D. Kuhn, R.S. Siegler, W. Damon and R.M. Lerner, *Handbook of Child Psychology: Cognition, Perception, and Language* (6th ed., pp. 687–733). Hoboken, NJ: John Wiley & Sons.

Gilmore, J., Knickmeyer, R. and Gao, W. (2018) Imaging structural and functional brain development in early childhood. *Natural Reviews Neuroscience*, 19(3), 123–137.

Gopnik, A., Griffiths, T.L. and Lucas, C.G. (2015) When younger learners can be better (or at least more open-minded) than older ones. *Current Directions in Psychological Science*, 24(2), 87–92.

Gopnik, A., Sobel, D.M., Schulz, L.E. and Glymour, C. (2001) Causal learning mechanisms in very young children: Two-, three-, and four-year-olds infer causal relations from patterns of variation and covariation. *Developmental Psychology*, 37(5), 620–629.

Gura, P. (1992) *Exploring learning: Young Children and Blockplay*. London: Sage.

Hansel, R. (2017) *Creative Block Play: A Comprehensive Guide to Learning through Building*. St Paul, MN: Redleaf Press.

Haylock, D. and Cockburn, A. (2008) *Understanding Mathematics for Young Children: A Guide for Foundation Stage and Lower Primary Teachers*. London: Sage.

Hirsch, E.D. (1996) *The Schools We Need and Why We Don't Have Them*. New York: Doubleday.

Krajewski, K. and Schneider, W. (2009) Early development of quantity to number–word linkage as a precursor of mathematical school achievement and mathematical difficulties: Findings from a four-year longitudinal study. *Learning and Instruction*, 19, 513–526.

Levine, S.C., Suriyakham, L.W., Rowe, M.L., Huttenlocher, J. and Gunderson, E.A. (2011) 'What counts in the development of young children's number knowledge?': Correction to Levine et al. (2010). *Developmental Psychology*, 47(1), 302.

Lubinski, D. (2013) Early spatial reasoning predicts later creativity and innovation, especially in STEM fields. *Science Daily*. Available at: www.sciencedaily.com/releases/2013/07/130715070347.htm [Accessed 1 January 2024].

Newcombe, N. (2010) Picture this: Increasing math and science learning by improving spatial thinking. *American Educator*, 34(2), 29–43.

Pollman, M.J. (2010) *Blocks and Beyond: Strengthening Early Math and Science Skills through Spatial Learning*. Baltimore, MD: Brookes.

Skene, K., O'Farrelly, C., Byrne, E. Kirby, N., Stevens, E.C. and Ramchandari, P.G. (2022) Can guidance during play enhance children's learning and development in educational contexts? A systematic review and meta-analysis. *Journal of Child Development*, 94(4), 1162–1180.

Tucker, K. (2014) *Mathematics Through Play in the Early Years*. London: Sage.

Williams, H.J. (2022) *Playful Mathematics for Children 3 to 7*. London: Sage.

Winter, R. (1992) 'Mathophobia', Pythagoras and roller-skating. In N. Nickson and S. Lerman, *The Social Context of Mathematics Education: Theory and Practice*. London: Southbank Press.

9

UNDERSTANDING THE WORLD, WELLBEING AND GLOBAL CITIZENSHIP

> *Young children experience their world as an environment of relationships, and these relationships affect virtually all aspects of their development.*
>
> National Scientific Council on the Developing Child, 2004

INTRODUCTION

Although all areas of learning are interconnected and the specific areas are supposed to be of equal importance, since the introduction of the Good Level of Development (GLD) as a measure of attainment in the EYFS, there has been a tendency in some settings to sideline the areas of learning that are not included in the measure. As far back as the 1950s, Drucker noted that we measure what we value and we value what we measure.

Ruth sometimes joins leaders in pupil progress meetings and the focus tends to be on how children are progressing in the prime areas and the specific areas of literacy and maths (those areas which inform the GLD); in the past, it has been rare for anyone to discuss *understanding the world*. I sometimes feel a sense of unease that although 'all areas of learning are important and interconnected' (DfE, 2024) some appear to be more important than others.

Anecdotally, I have noticed over the years that, as children progress through the school into Key Stage 1, some of the children who have achieved the GLD don't always achieve the expected standards in Key Stage 1, and one area where this has been particularly noticeable has been in literacy. This is where the interconnectedness of the goals becomes apparent. In order to be able to meet the expected standard as a reader in Key Stage 1, a child needs to be able to infer, to deduce, to predict and, in order to do this, a child needs to understand what it is they are reading about.

> Children build on their experiences, the wider and deeper their experience, the greater potential they have for secure development.
>
> (Early Years Coalition, 2021, p. 19)

If children have limited experience of what they are reading about, making sense of the text becomes a greater challenge. The DfE recognised this when they rewrote the educational programmes in 2020.

> As well as building important knowledge, this extends their familiarity with words that support understanding across domains. Enriching and widening children's vocabulary will support later reading comprehension.
>
> (DfE, 2024)

Of course, there is so much more that children gain from learning about their world and their role within it, but, at the same time, I am grateful that this acknowledgement has led to some deeper discussions about the purpose of understanding the world and it is beginning to come out of the shadows as the 'poor relation' to the specific areas of maths and literacy.

WHY UNDERSTANDING THE WORLD MATTERS

We've already established the connections between understanding the world and literacy, but the relationship to other areas of learning extends further. If children are truly to develop a sense of their unique self, they need to understand how they fit into the world, their role within it, how their actions impact upon others and how other people may live in similar or different ways to them. In this sense a child's sense of self and their personal, social and emotional development is directly linked to understanding the world. Very young children are quite egocentric and don't yet have 'theory of mind', they find it difficult to understand that others think differently to the way that they do. By introducing children to the lives of others, both in the past and present, they begin to understand the diversity of life and nature and to understand that they are part of a much bigger picture. This journey towards global citizenship starts with the child at the heart, and with the support and guidance from skilled adults who introduce them to experiences, ideas and resources to challenge and further their understanding.

THE GOALS ARE NOT THE CURRICULUM

Following the EYFS review of the curriculum in 2018, a group of 24 schools trialled the use of the new ELGs. These 'pilot' schools were monitored as part of an Education Endowment Foundation (EEF) research project to measure the impact of the reforms. The EEF study noted that:

> There was some confusion about whether or not the ELGs constitute 'the curriculum'. Given this confusion, further guidance about the nature of the ELGs as an assessment tool rather than defining the early years curriculum may be necessary when the revised ELGs are rolled out.
>
> (EEF, 2019)

However, as the reforms have become embedded, it has become quite clear that for staff working in Reception classes, the goals have to be borne in mind alongside the educational programme. Failure to take the goals into consideration when planning will make it challenging for some children to achieve the goals at the end of the Foundation Stage. Understanding the world is a unique area in this respect. With all other areas, I advise settings and schools not to look at the goals when thinking about building their curriculum, but to focus on the educational programmes. Looking at the goals can lead to a very narrow focus and opportunities to develop children's understanding could be missed in pursuit of the desired end result.

The specific nature of the goals here means that they will need to be taken into consideration. We still need to remember that the goals are the end point in the summer term in Reception, and to ensure that our curriculum remains broad and reflects the needs, ages and stages of the children in our care.

THE CHILD VERSUS THE CURRICULUM

Due to the nature of the reforms and the links to the Key Stage 1 curriculum, it can be easy to overlook the overarching principle of the unique child when planning for this area of learning. Nutbrown and Clough make the case for children's agency in planning:

> If current objectives in early years policy in relation to inclusion and citizenship in England are to be realised; [*sic*] identity and self-esteem are the two most important issues to be addressed. If children are successfully to experience a sense of inclusivity and belonging in their early years curriculum and pedagogy must attend to aspects of practice that make all children feel valued by enabling them to contribute their ideas and know that their contributions matter.
>
> (Nutbrown and Clough, 2009)

Plans are sometimes built from a 'top down' perspective in schools. The Key Stage 1 curriculum is sometimes pushed down into the Foundation Stage in the name of 'ambition'. Superficially, this can appear to make sense. If children need to know something by the end of Key Stage 1, why not just teach it earlier so that they have more time to absorb it? But if the foundations of understanding aren't there then the knowledge taught is unlikely to make sense to the child and the understanding of the concepts could be superficial at best. This was something the pilot schools discovered when trialling the ELGs.

> We thought we'd talk about Florence Nightingale, being a significant nurse from the past … We had all this stuff planned, it was all really exciting, but the children didn't get it, that it was from a long time ago … I don't know whether developmentally they weren't quite ready.
>
> (EEF, 2019)

At age four and five children's understanding of time, and 'a long time ago' can be variable so it's important to consider what will be meaningful to the children and how they can fit it into their understanding of time.

It is essential to consider where the child is at the moment, what funds of knowledge do they bring to us? What are their interests? What are their strengths?

If we think about the example above, we have to unpick the key components children need to understand before they are able to understand Florence Nightingale and the reason we still talk about her today.

Children need to understand the role of a nurse and what they do.

They need to understand that a long time ago medicine and nursing practices were very different to modern medicine.

They need to understand the passage of time, that a long time ago with respect to Florence Nightingale wasn't last week, or a few months ago at Christmas time, or before their birthday or even last year, which feels like 'a long time ago'. But that it was well before they were born, and their parents, grandparents and great grandparents were born.

When we look at this concept from the perspective of a four-year-old (as most of the children were when this topic was introduced) it is clear to see that it might be quite abstract and challenging for children to understand. This doesn't mean that we shouldn't share stories about people from the past, and talk about why we remember them, but we need to remember that unless these subjects are meaningful and relevant to children and they have an understanding of certain key concepts, it's unlikely they'll develop a real understanding of their significance.

This brings us neatly to our next question,

WHY?

If something is to take up precious space and time in our curriculum, we need to be able to identify why it is important and why it's important to teach it now. What is the purpose of teaching it? It's vital that we discuss these things as a team and if we're working in schools beyond the Early Years team and with curriculum leaders.

What do we want the children to know by the time they leave us? How can we ensure that the curriculum supports the child with their learning and development and is relevant to them?

WHAT'S YOUR VISION FOR UNDERSTANDING THE WORLD?

It's important to discuss what success looks like with the people who are working every day with the children. Is there an agreed vision for the children? Research into the study of early education and development (SEED) identifies that where leaders have a clear vision and everyone understands what success looks like, children achieve more. So, time spent discussing what a successful learner will look like is time well spent.

REFLECTION 9.1

If we look at the educational programme for *understanding the world* what will that look like for our children?

What is a successful learner?

What knowledge, skills and understanding do we want them to have?

How do we want them to use these skills?

How do we want them to be as citizens?

As Dr Julian Grenier stated in his *TES* column, September 2022:

> Planning an Early Years Curriculum that includes the Geography children will be learning in term two, week three in Reception, for example, is not sensible. It is useful to have a big picture of the learning children need to acquire from their time in the EYFS, but we must also remember the importance of *motivation, building on children's interests and learning through play*. There is plenty of evidence to support play based learning in the early years … play is at the heart of an effective Early Education.
>
> (Grenier, 2022, emphasis added)

So, we need to have a clear idea of what the big picture will look like so that we know what knowledge, skills and understanding we want the children to have when they leave us, but we shouldn't plan so much content that there is no room for agency and no opportunity for children to follow their interests and become more deeply involved in areas which interest them.

PROXIMAL TO DISTAL

When we think about early child development it is easy to see how children develop proximally to distally in their physical development. We know that children develop from the core outwards, with the control of our most distant body parts occurring last (see Chapter 6). I find it helpful to think about children's understanding of their wider world in the same way.

Tiny babies' worlds are very small, everything is new and their vision is still immature. Their immediate world focuses on themselves and their main caregiver(s). They will sometimes be soothed by a caregiver's voice and they seek their main caregiver's gaze. Gradually they begin to focus on their hands and feet as they become aware of them. As they develop and grow, they become more aware of others in the world; from three months babies are exploring their surroundings by moving their heads and will reach for objects in their sight lines, eventually picking them up and mouthing them. Thus, the baby is starting to make sense of the world around them. When we consider the ELGs and the expectations of what children will know, understand and do, it is staggering how much development takes place in the 60 months from birth. By the time children leave the Foundation Stage we expect them to know about people, places and events that are familiar to them, but also to be aware that there are people and places in the world that they don't know, that there are people who live totally different lives to them and that their actions impact on the lives of others. We expect them to understand the passage of time and that things have changed, and to make sense of timelines when their concept and understanding of time is still developing. It is, therefore, essential that we think about these things from the child's perspective and consider how what we are teaching relates to what they already understand. Babies are born with an innate drive to explore and discover the world around them, but at the same time many things they learn and understand in their earliest days are as a result of the interactions with supportive adults.

We need to build from where the children are right now, and then extend their understanding outward. This is the joy of Early Years teaching; the world is fascinating, exciting and new, and our job is to introduce the children to what the world has to offer.

WHERE ARE WE NOW?

The impact of the significant changes in society over the last few years cannot be understated. We are working with a Statutory Framework that was written before the Covid-19 pandemic, the international conflicts and the impact of austerity and cost of living crises that affect many of our communities.

But we are working with children who have experienced at least some and maybe all of these issues. Children and their families do not exist in a vacuum – in his *ecological systems theory* Urie Bronfenbrenner describes how humans are affected by an interconnected system with many different parts or 'environments for human development' (Bronfenbrenner, 1979, p. 8). He discussed the processes and conditions that have an impact on them at different times. The theory, drawn as a series of concentric rings or 'circles of influence', can help as we consider the different influences which impact on our children's lives (see Figure 9.1).

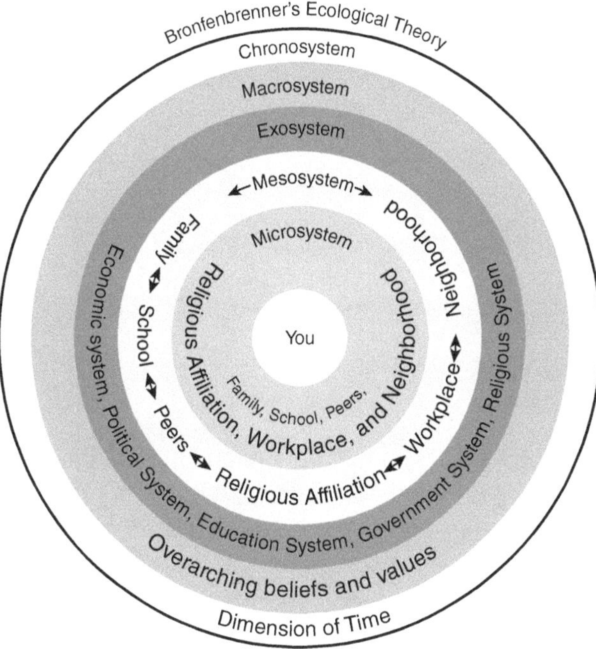

Figure 9.1 Bronfenbrenner's ecological systems theory

We are currently seeing the impact of many external factors on the children we work with in our settings.

REFLECTION 9.2

If we were to think about the 'circles of influence' currently impacting on our children and their families, what would we put in the concentric circles? What has changed and shifted over the past few years?

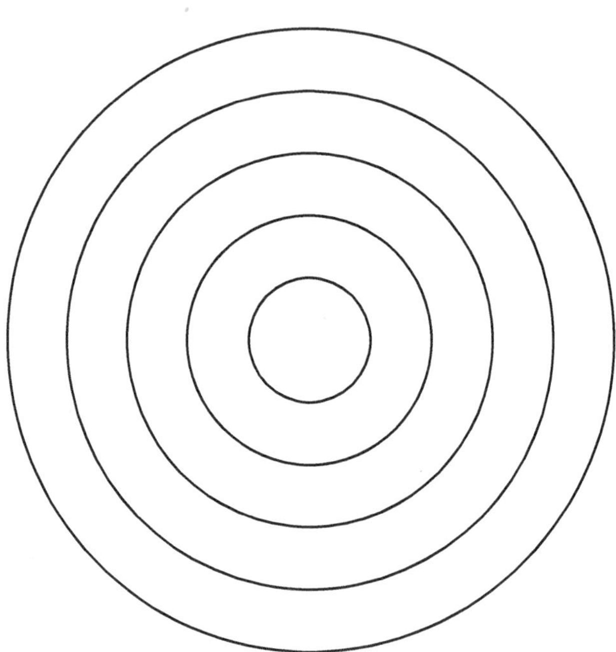

Figure 9.2 Blank example of circles of influence

While we must ensure that we meet the statutory requirements of the Early Years Foundation Stage Framework, we would be foolish not to acknowledge the impact of the pandemic on our children's lives.

Table 9.1 Age at which Covid-19 pandemic started based on year of birth

Year of birth	Age at start of pandemic
2013	From age 7
2014	From age 6
2015	From age 5
2016	From age 4
2017	From age 3
2018	From age 2
2019	From 12 months
2020	Born during pandemic
2021	Born during pandemic
2022	Born in aftermath of pandemic
2023	Born in aftermath of pandemic
2024	Born in aftermath of pandemic

REFLECTION 9.3

It is important to think about and discuss how your children's lives may have been affected by recent events. The children we have in our settings today are very different from the children we had four years ago. There will be no child in an Early Years setting who has had a 'typical' upbringing. Their experiences will have been different and this will impact on what we might need to provide for them or teach them.

Some important things to consider:

How was the child's early socialisation affected?

Could they attend baby and toddler groups?

Did they see relatives beyond their own immediate family when they were very young?

What opportunities did they have to learn to play alongside others, to meet different people?

What experiences have they had?

Did/do the children visit places such as shops, cafés, libraries, museums, galleries, zoos, parks, etc.?

How much time have they spent outdoors in nature?

There are other factors which might have affected children's early life and understanding of the world: austerity and the numerous cuts to services, leading to delays in identification of additional needs and support; conflict which may have affected their family or relatives; the cost of living crisis may mean that families haven't been out and enjoyed visits or holidays and for some children will mean that they have not experienced a lot of the things we might take for granted; the staffing crisis in our settings and services may mean that children have not formed attachments with a key person due to more frequent changes of staffing. We might also consider the impact of the 'top down' pressure many people working in Early Years now feel to move towards a more formal approach sooner and to focus on certain aspects of the curriculum perceived to be held in higher esteem by Ofsted, at the expense of others. All of these factors may impact on children's understanding of their world.

HOW DO WE OVERCOME THE MULTIPLE CHALLENGES TO DEVELOP CHILDREN'S UNDERSTANDING OF THEMSELVES AS GLOBAL CITIZENS?

It is helpful to return to the educational programme here:

> The frequency and range of children's personal experiences increases their knowledge and sense of the world around them – from visiting parks, libraries and museums to meeting important members of society such as police officers, nurses and firefighters.
>
> In addition, listening to a broad selection of stories, non-fiction, rhymes and poems will foster their understanding of our culturally, socially, technologically and ecologically diverse world.
>
> (DfE, 2024)

Think about the range of experiences and opportunities we can provide for our children within the context of our own community and the three strands within understanding the world.

PEOPLE, CULTURE AND COMMUNITIES

Consider what is available on the doorstep of your community. Remember children's understanding of people starts with them, their immediate family, their wider community, their setting, nursery or school, their local area and then beyond. Proximal to distal.

When working with young children we start by finding out about themselves and their families, their friends, religious and cultural communities; we also need to talk about our setting as a community so that children can understand that they are part of a community when they are at nursery or school. We need to be explicit about this so that children are fully aware of the different communities they are involved in. We can also explore the wider school or setting community, walking around the building and meeting people who do different jobs.

The next step is to look at the local area; a walk in the locality can reveal much about the children's understanding of their immediate community. Wherever possible, children need to see their own culture reflected in the setting and classroom, as well as a range of other cultures.

Dr Rudine Sims Bishop coined the term 'mirrors and windows', meaning children should be able to see themselves in their setting, in the resources, texts and curriculum, but should also be exposed to a diverse and rich range of communities and cultures and other opportunities – windows to a wider world. Texts and technology can be used to introduce children to wider experiences if budgets are constrained. It is essential that texts and resources are selected carefully and that cultural stereotypes are avoided. These are important considerations when developing our curriculum.

PAST AND PRESENT

Think about children's understanding of the passage of time. For our youngest children, history is what happened ten minutes ago, and we can build an understanding of time simply by using a visual timetable. We can talk about 'earlier today', 'this morning', 'this afternoon' and 'later on' so that this becomes a normal part of children's routine. By introducing the vocabulary in a meaningful way children will understand the context and begin to understand how time passes. We can then introduce vocabulary such as tomorrow and yesterday, and talk about things that happened 'in the past' in a meaningful way.

One of the most simple but meaningful ways of developing children's understanding of the passage of time is to build a timeline in the classroom. As significant events happen – for example, the first day of school, an autumn walk, harvest festival, Halloween, Divali, etc. – a photograph is added to the timeline, thus children can see how the passage of time is represented on the timeline and adults can talk about what happened in the past and in the future. In some settings a few key events from the previous room are copied and added to the beginning of the timeline for the next room, to give children a sense of continuity. In one school this was carried on into Key Stages 1 and 2, and significant historical events were added to the timeline to show where they fit in relation to the children's lives.

Children enjoy talking about their own personal history, how they have changed since they were a baby. This can then progress on to their family history, how things have changed since their parents were children; the school history or local history can be of interest to children in Reception as long as it is meaningful and relevant to them. They can talk about how the place they live in has changed by looking at old photographs.

THE NATURAL WORLD

Many Early Years theorists recognise the importance of children's innate connection with nature. The *nursery garden* was central to Froebel's kindergarten, a place where children could grow, learn and develop at their own pace, alongside adults who cultivate their learning. The McMillan sisters were firm believers in the benefits of outdoor learning and pioneered outdoor nurseries, opening the first in Deptford in 1914. Dewey, Montessori, Steiner, Reggio, McNeel and Russell (founders of the forest school movement) and countless other pioneers and theorists identify the importance of nature and being outdoors in shaping children's learning.

> Since nature provides such rich and varied sensory stimuli, it is perhaps not surprising that nature experiences have been associated with improved physical health and development, psychological well-being and cognitive functioning in children.
>
> (Ernst and Burcak, 2019, p. 4216)

Of course, some settings are at a greater advantage when it comes to supporting children's developing understanding of the natural world than others. If you're working in a space where there is limited outdoor space and little or no green space, then it will be more challenging. Some settings are fortunate to have large grounds, forests and orchards; others have to make do with visiting parks. In one school I work with the accessible green space is a cemetery. We work with what we have.

Remember children are naturally curious about nature, and understanding the natural world also includes understanding the properties of materials such as soil, sand, water, clay, etc. – all of which can be explored both indoors and outside. Pointing out and naming different weather types, observing and discussing changes in the weather, seasonal walks to explore sights, sounds, smells and temperatures are all accessible ways for children to make sense of the natural world around them.

If you are lucky enough to have a space where children can grow and plant seeds then do make use of it. From a very early age children are fascinated by the creatures and plants in the garden and we should capitalise on this interest. But if there is no outdoor space then make space indoors or in the entrance to the building with containers; seeds can be grown in simple trays. A bug hotel can be placed strategically outside the door to encourage insects so that children have the opportunity to look at creatures closely, and to understand that they must be handled with care.

> There is a growing body of research to demonstrate that children's positive early experiences in natural environments support them in developing knowledge of nature, scientific thinking, and dispositions (respect and an ethic of care) that are the foundation of environmental literacy skills, and shape their motivation to become agents for environmental change.
>
> (Education Hub, 2021)

REFLECTION 9.4

How does your curriculum reflect the unique needs of your children?

Does your curriculum provide windows to the wider world as well as reflecting your community?

Are the links between children's personal, social and emotional development and their sense of self fully embedded in your *understanding the world* curriculum?

How can you provide children with hands-on, meaningful experiences in your setting?

KEY POINTS OF THE CHAPTER

Understanding the world needs to start from the child, not the Key Stage 1 curriculum.

Look at the educational programme from the child's perspective; what do they already know and understand?

Build on the rich experiences already in your local community.

Ensure your curriculum and resources provide mirrors and windows.

REFERENCES

Bronfenbrenner, U. (1979) *The Ecology of Human Development: Experiments by Nature and Design*. Cambridge, MA: Harvard University Press.

Department for Education (DfE) (2024) *Early Years Foundation Stage (EYFS) Statutory Framework*. Available at: www.gov.uk/government/publications/early-years-foundation-stage-framework--2 [Accessed 1 January 2024].

Early Years Coalition (2021) *Birth to 5 Matters Non-statutory Guidance to the Early Years Foundation Stage*. Available at: https://birthto5matters.org.uk/wp-content/uploads/2021/03/Birthto5Matters-download.pdf [Accessed 1 January 2024].

Education Endowment Foundation (EEF) (2019) *Early Years Foundation Stage Profile Pilot*. Available at: https://educationendowmentfoundation.org.uk/projects-and-evaluation/projects/early-years-foundation-stage-profile-pilot [Accessed 3 April 2024].

Education Hub (2021) Curriculum and pedagogy in the outdoors. *Education Hub*. Available at: https://theeducationhub.org.nz/curriculum-and-pedagogy-in-the-outdoors/ [Accessed 13 June 2024].

Ernst, J. and Burcak, F. (2019) Young children's contributions to sustainability: The influence of nature play on curiosity, executive function skills, creative thinking, and resilience. *Sustainability*, 11(15), 4212–4234.

Grenier, J. (2022) Why we need a mongrel curriculum in EYFS. *Times Educational Supplement*, 23 September. Available at: www.tes.com/magazine/teaching-learning/early-years/why-we-need-mongrel-curriculum-eyfs [Accessed 1 January 2024].

National Scientific Council on the Developing Child (2004) Young children develop in an environment of relationships. Working Paper No. 1. Available at: www.developingchild.net [Accessed 1 February 2024].

Nutbrown, C. and Clough, P. (2009) Citizenship and inclusion in the Early Years: Understanding and responding to children's perspectives on 'belonging'. *International Journal of Early Years Education*, 17(3), 191–206.

10

EXPRESSIVE ARTS AND DESIGN

A place to represent the world in many different ways ...
A place for creativity, imagination and exploration ...
Of provocations and challenges
Of tenacity and problem solving.

'Atelier' by Patricia Hunter-McGrath

INTRODUCTION

In the previous chapter we touched upon the fact that only two of the specific areas of the EYFS (DfE, 2024) are part of the GLD judgement, and how this can lead to the other two being side-lined and perhaps given less prominence in the curriculum. Although the arts and creativity have always played a central and crucial role in early childhood education, anecdotally, they rarely feature in discussions during pupil progress meetings because they do not feature as part of the GLD. This doesn't mean that they are not vital for children's learning and wellbeing.

Creativity and exploration of different media have formed a significant part of many Early Years pedagogies and have been central to the beliefs of a number of theorists over the years.

Reggio Emilia nurseries each have an *atelier studio*, which is an area equipped with a variety of open-ended materials that gives children a chance to explore, experiment, express themselves, make mistakes, follow through an idea, plan and then create and share ideas with their peers. The studio offers a variety of ways for children to interact and explore without fear of making mistakes; there is no correct way to do something. This allows children to find their own ways of working, their own preferred materials to use and their own ideas to follow.

> Our image of the child is rich in potential, strong, powerful, competent and, most of all connected to adults and other children.
>
> (Loris Malaguzzi, 1994)

One of Froebel's key principles was *creativity and the power of symbols*. He also encouraged 'freedom with guidance', allowing children to explore their natural fascinations, make choices, pursue their own talents and express themselves freely, and to learn to persevere when things are challenging.

Froebelian practice also includes a number of 'occupations' for young children. Weaving, paper-folding, clay, construction, woodwork, sewing, paper-pricking, sticks and peas for construction allow children to develop their creative skills, express themselves in a variety of ways and build resilience and precision. Many of the resources we see in settings today such as block play, clay, treasure baskets, loose parts, woodwork, etc. can be traced back to Froebelian principles.

Visit most Early Years settings, play groups and toddler groups and you will usually find a creative or craft area. It's highly likely that, if you're lucky, somewhere there will be an adult who treasures a piece of your artwork from your early childhood. Creative areas allow children to express themselves freely and give us insights into how they see the world and see themselves in the world.

CREATIVE DEVELOPMENT OR EXPRESSIVE ARTS AND DESIGN?

Historically, within the curriculum this area of learning has changed since its original iteration as Creative Development when the educational programme stated that:

> Children's creativity must be extended by the provision of support for their curiosity, exploration and play. They must be provided with opportunities to explore and share their thoughts, ideas and feelings, for example, through a variety of art, music, movement, dance, imaginative and role-play activities, mathematics, and design and technology.
>
> (Pascal et al., 2018)

Although the change in name might seem insignificant, in the last few years we have witnessed an increasing trend in favour of more adult-directed approaches towards the expressive arts and design (EAD); in some settings the focus has shifted from process to product.

The 2024 educational programme states:

> It is important that children have regular opportunities to engage with the arts, enabling them to explore and play with a wide range of media and materials. The quality and variety of what children see, hear and participate in is crucial for developing their understanding, self-expression, vocabulary and ability to communicate through the arts. The frequency, repetition and depth of their experiences are fundamental to their progress in interpreting and appreciating what they hear, respond to and observe.
>
> (DfE, 2024, p. 11)

In the new framework it could be argued that the arts have become more of a vehicle for other areas of learning, particularly when we look at the goal which relates to narratives and storytelling. The educational programme states clearly that children should be able to explore and play with a wider range of media and materials, but the rise in the use of published schemes means that many of the children's experiences in EAD are becoming adult-led. There is of course an important balance to be achieved. We need to teach children key skills so that they are able to use tools, materials and resources effectively, but we must also ensure that we do not lose sight of the importance of allowing children to express themselves freely using a range of different media and materials. Several studies have found that educational environments in which children view themselves to have some level of control and that allow for free choice in activities and collaborative learning have been shown to produce higher levels of creativity (Amabile and Gitomer, 1984; Ryan and Grolnick, 1986).

The challenge is to strike the balance between adult-led and child-initiated expression. In 2013, Cathy Nutbrown conducted a critical review of the international literature relating to the place of Early Years arts education. Her analysis of arts-based learning concluded that young children's experiences in art have not been nurtured in ways which support their naturally artistically attuned development. Nutbrown also identifies the need to provide more adult role models as artists. She argues that, because young children's response to the world is primarily sensory and aesthetic, the Early Years curriculum should give due attention to the arts (Nutbrown, 2013). There is an urgent need to better conceptualise ways of working with young children in relation to the arts. There is a growing interest in arts-based educational research (ABER), but this is not yet as strong in early childhood education. In fact, in their 2019 research review, Pascal et al. noted 'Given the shortage of evidence from studies in relation to this area of learning, we looked at the evidence presented in recent wider reviews of evidence' (p. 48).

It seems we know instinctively that the arts matter, and we can make the links to other areas of the curriculum, but research in this field is yet to catch up with the research in other areas of learning. It is possible that this is because arts-based outcomes are more challenging to quantify.

> No test, no observational schedule, no checklist, will adequately uncover the richness of children's minds and hearts, but, we suggest, arts-based responses to critical research questions about childhood and children's learning can take us nearer to a more meaningful portrayal of what it is to be a child and a young learner.
>
> (Clough and Nutbrown, 2019, p. 3)

So what does this mean for those working with children every day?

It may mean that we face 'top down' pressure to make our EAD curriculum align or even emulate the Key Stage 1 curriculum.

It may mean that EAD remains the poor relation of the EYFS and is squeezed from the curriculum because other aspects are seen as more important, with a clear research base and easily measurable outcomes.

It may mean that we have to find new ways to be creatively compliant, to justify EAD as part of our everyday offer. One of the ways we can do this is by promoting the impact it has not just on children's outcomes in EAD, but on their wellbeing, on their ability to focus and concentrate and on their outcomes in other areas of the curriculum.

HOW CREATIVITY LINKS WITH OTHER AREAS OF THE CURRICULUM

As we have explored in other areas of learning, there is considerable overlap between the different areas. Within EAD we can see opportunities for children to develop and express their understanding of the world, to show us how they see themselves and others in the world and to explore their representations in two or three dimensions.

Barnes and Shirley (2007) encourage us to support children to consider how different aspects of learning can be made 'strangely familiar', by encouraging the children to explore and express their interpretations using painting, poetry and music. In this approach the teacher acts as facilitator, providing relevant resources and presenting children with different perspectives, but the control is handed to the children. So they might focus on an aspect of understanding the world, such as the local area or their classroom, and express their likes and dislikes using digital media – film, photography, stories, dance, art, shows, sculpture, etc.

Often EAD provides an outlet for children who may find more traditional forms of recording and expression more challenging.

One of the questions we posed in Chapter 4, 'Communication and language', as part of the appreciative inquiry was 'Where do you hear children talking a lot?' When I ask this question in training or working with practitioners in settings and schools, I'm frequently told that workshop areas, art and creative areas, junk-modelling and dough areas are spaces where a lot of conversation happens. Often when children are engaged in creative activities they will chatter with their friends, sometimes about their creations, sometimes about other things. Opportunities to play with musical instruments, to sing and listen to different music are all excellent ways to develop children's early language and communication skills. Young children are still developing their auditory discrimination and playing with instruments can help them attune to different sounds.

Loose parts play and large construction, block play and construction kits are also often areas where there is a lot of discussion; these open-ended resources not only develop children's creative thinking, but also support them with their mathematical understanding and spatial reasoning. Transient art is an excellent way to develop children's understanding of pattern, arrays and subitising. Patterning skills at age four are a better predictor of children's maths at age 11 than children's numerical understanding, according to Rittle-Johnson et al. (2016).

Sand, water, clay and mud play allow excellent opportunities to develop creative expression but also support children's mathematical thinking as well as their understanding of different materials and their properties.

EXPRESSIVE ARTS AND DESIGN AND PHYSICAL DEVELOPMENT

Many of the skills children need to produce their creations require the same skills as they develop when learning to write: manipulation of tools and objects, dexterity, fine motor control, the need for precision. Hand and muscle strength can be developed using clay, dough, plasticine, mud, tools, etc. When creating with larger construction kits or with found objects such as tyres, crates and planks, logs, etc. children will have to move heavy objects, developing their core strength, their upper body strength and their proprioception, all of which will help them when they need to write. Exploring with construction kits often develops children's fine motor skills and kits which involve twisting and turning motions will support rotor development in the wrists.

Different types of brushes and media, different surfaces to paint on, whether they are large, small, flat on the ground or table or vertically on an easel, board or wall will provide different types of motor development and the motivation to create can help children to overcome their anxieties around writing and mark-making.

ROLE PLAY

There has been a significant shift in the way role play is framed within the educational programmes and goals. The 2021 goals require children to:

> Express and communicate their ideas, thoughts and feelings by using a widening range of materials, suitable tools, imaginative and role play, movement, designing and making, and a variety of songs and musical instruments
>
> Use their imagination in art and design, music, dance, imaginative and role play and stories.
>
> (DfE, 2021)

These were replaced by 'Invent, adapt and recount narratives and stories with peers and their teacher' (DfE, 2024, p. 16).

This seems to frame the purpose of role play purely as a form of retelling narratives. While role play often involves narratives, it also involves so much more than retelling or creating stories.

In fact, when observed, much of the play in this area does not follow a story or narrative in the traditional sense. We notice that children will often participate quietly but intently in role play and this is a very important stage in the learning process. Young children, in the early stages of learning language and particularly those who are new to English, can often be observed intently observing play or joining in without speaking. This phase, known as 'intent participation' (Tabors, 2014) is a vital stage of children's language development.

Although it may seem pedantic to unpick the wording of the framework, we have to bear in mind that those who are inexperienced in working with young children may look at role play through a purely narrative lens, and it's essential that we are able to articulate all the other vital aspects of early learning that take place in the role play area. It is important that children have a range of role play opportunities and these goals are not interpreted as solely retelling stories with the teacher or which have been shared by the teacher.

Role play is a powerful tool to support children's learning. Guilfoyle and Mistry (2013) identified the importance of role play in improving the vocabulary of English as an additional language (EAL) learners and Whitebread and Bingham (2014) found that young children can reason, problem-solve and demonstrate cognitive flexibility in quite sophisticated ways when they are engaged in pretend play. Role play supports children's language development, personal and social skills, and executive functioning skills, and there is significant evidence to show that children who leave the Foundation Stage with well-developed executive function and self-regulation are well placed to achieve more in their learning than those who have not developed these vital skills. Whitebread et al. (2007) noted the frequent occurrence of children aged three to five demonstrating metacognitive and self-regulatory abilities when involved in playful activities, particularly in constructional and pretend play. Vallotton and Ayoub (2011) found that there was a strong relationship between children's vocabulary size at 14, 24 and 36 months and their self-regulatory behaviours, their ability to remain on task, to persevere, to adapt to changes and to the responses of others. As we know from Chapter 4, vocabulary size is a strong indicator of children's long-term outcomes.

By providing opportunities for children to engage in high-quality role play we are laying the groundwork for the development of self-regulation, problem-solving, pro-social behaviour and language development.

Bruner and Haste (2010) refer to children as 'meaning-makers' and we will often see children working through problems and trying to make sense of their world through well-developed role play and small-world areas.

WHAT DOES THIS MEAN FOR PRACTITIONERS WORKING WITH CHILDREN EVERY DAY?

There are no rules about the areas of learning that must be provided in the enabling environment (see Chapter 11, 'Learning environments'). However, it is worth reflecting on whether there are sufficient opportunities for children to enact different roles, make up narratives and tell stories.

I am a passionate advocate for domestic role play throughout the Foundation Stage. Over the last few years, increasing numbers of children have needed additional support to become confident communicators, so it makes sense to provide them with a role play area where things feel familiar to them. If we are to elicit conversations and serve and return interactions, we need to provide spaces where they will feel comfortable in this; for most children nowhere is more comfortable and familiar than home. With this in mind, we should try to provide a high-quality 'home' area that reflects what the children know. There has been a growing trend to provide 'retro' home areas which are aesthetically pleasing but do not always connect with children's experiences. I have played in beautifully recreated living rooms, which remind me of my grandma's house in the 1970s but did not connect with the children's experiences. When we discussed why the children were so quiet in this space, we realised that the living room is often a quiet space where we sit and read, or maybe watch television, and as this role play area contained neither resource, the children weren't quite sure what to do. By spending time in an area and considering how you might play there, what resources you might need to be successful, it is possible to identify how you can develop this area further. Consider where most of the talk happens in the home. Often there is a lot of discussion in the kitchen: what to eat, how to cook, washing, ironing, cleaning. Ensure that the resources available allow for meaningful purposeful play. It is also important to reflect children's own cultures as far as possible, without becoming tokenistic. It is helpful to involve children and families in equipping role play areas. One school I worked with had a range of diverse resources in the kitchen area, with cooking utensils that reflected the myriad of cultures represented in the classroom. This resulted in children demonstrating their skills with the different tools to their classmates. In an area with a significant traveller population, one of the role play areas became a wagon. In inner city areas with a number of children being housed in hostels and hotels staff have made role play areas that reflect the reality of everyday experiences for the children. Including photographs of the children and their carers in the role play areas can bring a homely touch and provide an opportunity for children to self-soothe or to co-regulate with an adult when they are missing someone.

If at all possible, we should have more than one role play area: one which reflects the home; and one which might relate to the children's current interests, or something which you've been teaching; or a more open-ended space where children can construct their own role play, although they may need support to do this at first. Shops, offices, hairdressers, doctors' surgeries can all provide opportunities to build children's understanding of their world. Ideally, children should have some experience of the type of space the role play represents, but this isn't always possible so support from adults to understand what happens in this place can really help to give children the confidence to play.

David Whitebread (2019) stated that role play is 'perhaps the most sophisticated type of play in which young children engage, and one that many children struggle to perform well. As such it is a prime example of where a skilful adult can participate, taking on some of the regulatory role' (p. 28). Where space is at a premium, having a domestic role play indoors and a different role play outdoors can overcome this issue. Den building, construction materials and cardboard boxes allow for a flexible approach to role playing. I have also used prop boxes to great effect with role play, a small collection of items that the children can transport to any space to make a role play area. This can allow for spontaneity and flexibility.

CASE STUDY 10.1

YONGHE ROAD KINDERGARTEN IN SHANGHAI

Taken from Aaron Bradbury and Matthew Northall's blog

The full blog can be found here: https://nottinghaminstituteofeducation.wordpress.com/2024/01/30/a-visit-to-a-shanghai-kindergarten/

The curriculum in Chinese kindergartens includes a mix of academic and social development. While there is some emphasis on early literacy and numeracy skills, the overall approach is often play-based, with an emphasis on fostering creativity, curiosity, and social skills, drawing some comparisons with the English Early Years Foundation Stage Statutory Framework. Whilst the connection to the work of Friedrich Froebel was evident in the Kindergarten approach in Shanghai, so was that of Loris Malaguzzi and the Reggio Emilia approach. The arts shone through both in the Kindergarten and at SXC. Both

(Continued)

locations had prominent performance spaces and teachers were actively encouraged to promote art, singing, dancing, and dramatic re-enactments. Within the Kindergarten there were a variety of dedicated art spaces (both indoors and outside) and the children took a genuine pride in what they had been working on.

A visiting art teacher attends the Kindergarten once a week and engages the children in a range of crafts ranging from collage production, painting, photography, traditional Chinese calligraphy and performing arts. This is not dissimilar in role to that of the Atelierista in Reggio settings. This term, the children were concentrating on the theme of autumn and we saw their work which adorned the walls of dedicated art rooms, like masterpieces hanging in the Louvre.

REFLECTION 10.1

- How do you value EAD in your Early Years setting?
- Do you ever look at how arts are valued and how they can be incorporated into your daily practices?
- Do you value the pictures? What do you do with them?
- Do you promote singing, drama and dancing?

What we took from visiting the settings in China is that it does not have to look perfect, feel perfect or look aesthetically pleasing to value what the children produced. Arts and expression need to have the time to add value to the other areas of learning too, without them all being intertwined and narrowed; this means that our children will thrive developmentally and be ready for their next stage of learning. We can achieve this by making sure that we give time equally to all areas of both prime and specific areas of development.

RESOURCING THE WORKSHOP/CREATIVE AREA

Much will depend on the space you have available for resources. Think carefully about how you will display these and how children will access them. Having too much of any item available at any one time can send the message that there's an inexhaustible supply and this can mean that children won't always look after the resources. Sometimes it's better to have less out, especially in the early stages of children learning to use the resources independently. This allows children to explore the resources without becoming overwhelmed and adults can support them as and when they need help. Gradually resources can be built up. There are no rules about what to have in a creative area, but think carefully about the tools you want children to be able to use, the skills and knowledge you want them to have by the time they leave you and plan accordingly.

MUSIC

We must ensure that children's experiences of music don't focus entirely on performance. Exposure to music, movement and singing should be a core part of everyday provision. Routines can be accompanied by songs; this gives a children a sense of being part of a group who have the same shared values and experiences. Music can also provide cues for children who find following verbal instructions more challenging. Singing songs, playing with sounds, tuning into different instruments and exploring them together are all important skills for developing auditory discrimination, a vital component of early reading. Select instruments carefully and teach children how to use them and look after them.

If we examine all the areas of learning that are supported by EAD, we can see how essential it is for children's overall development. It really does pack a pedagogical punch! On top of that it gives children agency, opportunities to express themselves, to experiment and develop strong characteristics of effective learning.

REFLECTION 10.2

How much time is spent on EAD in your setting at the moment?

Are the arts valued?

Does everyone working with the children understand how EAD interconnects with other areas of learning?

How can you plan for the right balance of teaching techniques and approaches and giving children creative freedom?

How much time do adults spend in role play with children?

KEY POINTS OF THE CHAPTER

EAD supports children's learning and development across all domains.

It is essential to consider the skills and knowledge you want children to develop in this area of learning.

Role play is fundamental to children's learning and should be about more than just a narrative.

Children should have opportunities to explore freely and express themselves without having to focus on an end product.

REFERENCES

Amabile, T.M. and Gitomer, J. (1984) Children's artistic creativity. *Personality and Social Psychology Bulletin*, 10(2), 209–215.

Barnes, J. and Shirley, I. (2007) Strangely familiar: Cross-curricular and creative thinking in teacher education. *Improving Schools*, 10(20), 162–179.

Bruner, J. and Haste, M. (2010) *Making Sense* (Routledge Revivals) [Preprint]. London: Routledge. doi:10.4324/9780203830581.

Clough, P. and Nutbrown, C. (2019) Exploring the place of arts-based approaches in early childhood education research. *Journal of Early Childhood Research*, 17(1), 3–13.

Department for Education (DfE) (2021) *Development Matters: Non-Statutory Curriculum Guidance for the Early Years Foundation Stage*. Available at: https://assets.publishing.service.gov.uk/media/64e6002a20ae890014f26cbc/DfE_Development_Matters_Report_Sep2023.pdf [Accessed 1 January 2024].

DfE (2024) *Early Years Foundation Stage (EYFS) Statutory Framework*. Available at: www.gov.uk/government/publications/early-years-foundation-stage-framework--2 [Accessed 9 February 2024].

Guilfoyle, N. and Mistry, M. (2013) How effective is role play in supporting speaking and listening for pupils with English as an additional language in the Foundation Stage? *Education 3–13*, 41(1), 63–70.

Malaguzzi, L. (1994) Your image of the child: Where teaching begins. *Exchange*, 96, 52–56.

Nutbrown, C. (2013) Conceptualising arts-based learning in the Early Years. *Research Papers in Education*, 28(2), 239–263.

Pascal, C., Bertram T. and Peckham K. (2018) *DfE Review of Evidence on EYFS Early Learning Goals, Teaching Content and Pedagogy in Reception Year*. DfE: London.

Pascal, C., Bertram, T. and Rouse, L. (2019) *Getting it Right in the Early Years Foundation Stage: A Review, Early Education*. Available at: www.early-education.org.uk/getting-it-right-early-years-foundation-stage-review-evidence [Accessed 6 January 2024].

Rittle-Johnson, B., Fyfe, E.R., Hofer, K.G. and Farran, D.C. (2016) Early math trajectories: Low-income children's mathematics knowledge from ages 4 to 11. *Child Development*, 88(5), 1727–1742.

Ryan, R.M. and Grolnick, W.S. (1986) Origins and pawns in the classroom: Self-report and projective assessments of individual differences in children's perceptions. *Journal of Personality and Social Psychology*, 50(3), 550–558.

Tabors, P.O. (2014) One child, two languages: A guide for early childhood educators of children learning English as a second language. *Education Review* [Preprint]. doi:10.14507/er.v0.1064.

Vallotton, C. and Ayoub, C. (2011) Use your words: The role of language in the development of toddlers' self-regulation. *Early Childhood Research Quarterly*, 26(2), 169–181.

Whitebread, D. (2019) Overview: The contribution of research in developmental psychology to early childhood education. In D. Whitebread, V. Grau, K. Kumpulainen, M.M. McClelland, N.E. Perry and D. Pino-Pasternak, *The Sage Handbook of Developmental Psychology and Early Childhood Education* (pp. 1–20). London: Sage. doi:10.4135/9781526470393.n1.

Whitebread, D. and Bingham, S. (2014) School readiness: Starting age, cohorts and transitions in the Early Years. In J. Moyles, J. Georgeson and J. Payler, *Early Years Foundations: Critical Issues* (2nd edn) (pp. 179–191). Berkshire: Open University Press.

Whitebread, D., Bingham, S., Grau, V., Pino Pasternak, D. and Sangster, C. (2007) Development of metacognition and self-regulated learning in young children: Role of collaborative and peer-assisted learning. *Journal of Cognitive Education and Psychology*, 6(3), 433–445.Case study 10.1

11

EARLY YEARS CURRICULUM AND PEDAGOGY

When we talk about pedagogy in the Early Years, we mean how we teach, or all the things that adults do to foster children's learning and development.

Early Education, 2022

INTRODUCTION

This chapter looks at the pedagogy and teaching needed within the Early Years. It will also discuss the main principles of Early Years Foundation Stage through the statutory and non-statutory frameworks and guidance. We are making no apologies that much of this chapter focuses on pedagogy of play, which includes teaching and opportunities developed for learning. The chapter makes it clear that the role of the adult is crucial in developing an environment which establishes positive relationships with children. We wanted to start with a quote from Ofsted which has helped us define teaching in the Early Years.

> Teaching is a broad term that covers the many different ways in which adults help young children learn. It includes their interactions with children during planned and child-initiated play and activities, communicating and modelling language, showing, explaining, demonstrating, exploring ideas, encouraging, questioning, recalling, providing a narrative for what they are doing, facilitating and setting challenges. It takes account of

> the equipment that adults provide, and the attention given to the physical environment, as well as the structure and routines of the day that establish expectations. Integral to teaching is how practitioners assess what children know, understand and can do, as well as taking account of their interests and dispositions to learn (characteristics of effective learning), and how practitioners use this information to plan children's next steps in learning and to monitor their progress.
>
> (Ofsted, 2021)

Furthermore, *Birth to 5 Matters: Non-statutory Guidance for the Early Years Foundation Stage* explains that an Early Years pedagogy should be based on:

> Warm, trusting relationships with knowledgeable adults support[ing] children's learning more effectively than any amount of resources. ... Follow the child's lead to the meeting of minds. ... Tuning in, observing and wondering come first. ... A knowledgeable practitioner can decide when to stand back, when to interact, and what to offer the child. ... Learning together with adults and with other children is important across all contexts.
>
> (Early Years Coalition, 2021, pp. 32–33)

Pedagogy refers to the process of educating. An instructional strategy is a set of instructional techniques and strategies designed to facilitate learning and provide opportunities for acquiring knowledge, skills, attitudes and dispositions within a particular social and material context. In this context, it refers to the interaction between teacher and learner as well as to the learning environment (Siraj-Blatchford et al., 2002).

It takes a great deal of effort and dedication to be an effective early childhood practitioner and educator. To ensure that all children make progress in their areas of learning and development – becoming more knowledgeable, skilled, thoughtful and confident – we continually reflect on and adapt what we do as we get to know and understand the children with whom we work. We need to be able to explain how we do this to staff, parents and carers, and the wider community, and one of the most important ways to do so is by recognising three key elements: *curriculum, pedagogy* and *assessment.*

Dubiel (2020) argues that curriculum, pedagogy and assessment are integral components of what we do, but they have separate functions.

Curriculum refers to the content, the knowledge that we wish children to possess. In our aspirations for our children, we all have expectations of what they should know and be able to accomplish. Typically, this is the combination of what a prescribed external curriculum – such as the English EYFS Statutory Framework – specifies as ELGs and what educators value and know children require in order to achieve their fullest potential.

Pedagogy is a pedagogical process, the method by which we teach children – or, in other words, the way in which the curriculum is delivered to them. The activities we conduct, the questions we ask, the conversations we have and even the materials we choose are all adapted to help shape a child's own way of learning.

Assessment is the means by which we can determine whether this approach is working, and whether we have a good understanding of the children on the level necessary to determine what 'curriculum' they need and what pedagogy will be most effective in delivering that curriculum (Dubiel, 2020).

PEDAGOGY AND PLAY

Children learn through play. It is the way in which they form friendships, how they formulate and test ideas, and how they make sense of their surroundings. The literature provides a wealth of information about how play facilitates learning. The provision of space for play, particularly in school settings where there is a tension between playful learning and the structure of most school curricula, is crucial.

Typically, play is seen as a pleasurable, spontaneous and non-goal-oriented activity that involves anticipation, flow and surprise (Barnett and Owens, 2015). According to Gray (2016), play is both objective and subjective, encompassing both qualities of observed behaviour and feelings experienced during play. The UN Committee on the Rights of the Child (2013) explains that play is associated with children and is essential to their holistic growth, learning and development. It is through play that children construct a sense of meaning about the world around them. Children's autonomy and independence within play are the central pillars of play (Tovey, 2020).

Playful learning experiences and practices are valued differently by educators, as is their understanding of the nature of play. It is possible for one educator to view play differently from another educator. It is also important to note that those of us who do see the value in play as a centralised opportunity to enhance learning also value the time, space and materials that accompany creating such a playful environment. Play can be misunderstood by those who view it as 'just play'. Children who engage in playful learning are more likely to be engaged in covering the curriculum and to bring joy to learning. Play pedagogy provides a systematic approach to learning and teaching through play. To change a school's culture to value play, the following need to be considered.

- How is play celebrated in the school or setting?
- Does the school examine and learn deeply about the value of play and the benefits this has for a child?
- Is play visible, acknowledged and shared across the school or setting?
- Does your setting and school provide up-to-date training and shared thinking to value and foster a playful environment?

As part of fostering a focus on play and changing mindsets, it is essential to create a culture that values its core elements. It is imperative that children are provided with an environment where they can take risks, learn from their mistakes, explore innovative ideas and feel joy.

REFLECTION 11.1

- How would you define play?
- What is needed for play in your Early Years setting? (People? Resources? Space?)

The UNCRC Article 31 states:

> Children's play is any behaviour, activity or process initiated, controlled, and structured by children themselves: it takes place whenever and wherever opportunities arise.
>
> (UN, 2013, p. 17)

Defining play has been a topic of ongoing discussion among academics – regarding what constitutes play and the circumstances in which it should take place. In addition, a child's definition of play and an adult's definition of play can differ considerably (McInnes et al., 2013). According to Eberle (2014, p. 214), play consists of six elements: anticipation, surprise, pleasure, understanding, strength, and poise. According to Eberle, play must be defined by children having fun. According to Bottrill (2018, p. 26), play is creativity and should be defined rather than provided with a definition. Play is closely aligned with the UNCRC's definition of play and affirms the importance of providing children with a safe, joyful environment in which they can explore their own concepts of learning.

WHY IS PLAY IMPORTANT?

Early childhood education settings today are influenced by the theories and practices of child development theorists. Despite the differences between the theories of Froebel, Vygotsky and Piaget regarding the definition of learning for children, they all share one focus: the importance of play. According to these theorists, play is described as an aspect of play rather than as a definition of what play is. No matter how you analyse these theorists' work, they all agree that play is fundamental to a child's learning and development, and that it is an innate and natural urge to explore and comprehend the world around them.

Neuroscience and the research that supports this claim have identified that children demonstrate higher levels of motivation, self-esteem and engagement, as well as higher levels of emotional well-being (McInnes et al., 2013). Additionally, play has a positive effect on brain development (Center on the Developing Child, 2021). In addition to providing opportunities for children to learn to interact with the environment, adults and other children, play also promotes the development of responsive relationships. As a result of these interactions through play, children can strengthen their connections between what they know and what they observe in the world around them. In the brain, neural connections establish the basis for learning, as well as establishing the basis for thinking, knowledge, behaviour and general life skills. As a result of interactions within the environment or with other individuals, what is known as a serve and return interaction is facilitated. By interacting with their world, children are able to make sense of their world through experiences that are rich in learning patterns that support their development.

A child can become more resilient through play when they can test out theories, take risks and solve problems in a safe environment without fear of failure.

CASE STUDY 11.1

TREVOR: EARLY YEARS TEACHER, RECEPTION CLASS

Trevor explains that he allows the class to have time where they do not have him or his teaching assistant interfering with their play, which means uninterrupted time where adults do not intervene. He explains that the activities which he puts out every day do not always have a theme; sometimes he explores things which would give children an opportunity to work together and problem-solve.

> We share the space with another Reception class, and it is important to make sure that all teachers and professionals within the unit have a clear understanding that certain areas of the classroom are for children to explore their own thinking. This has given us an opportunity to observe children while they are playing and has given us further encouragement to do things like focused phonics as they are enjoying having the time to just be and play. We all spread ourselves out across the provision so that we can see the enhancements being made by the children alongside the more focused activities which are teacher-led.

REFLECTION 11.2

1. Do you relate to the scenario that Trevor has given?
2. Do you have uninterrupted play where children are left to think, have times of trial and error and allow them to be engrossed in what they are doing?
3. Have you developed another system that allows children to access play through continuous provision?

EARLY YEARS CURRICULUM

In England and within the UK, we would argue that pedagogy and curriculum go hand in hand, so it would not be fair to discuss Early Years pedagogy without mentioning the Early Years curriculum. England is covered by the EYFS. In Scotland, there is a *Curriculum for Excellence for the Early Years* (Education Scotland, n.d.), in Wales there is a *Foundation Phase* (Welsh Government, 2015), and in Northern Ireland there is *Curriculum Guidance for Pre-School Education* (CEA, 2019).

An EYFS curriculum consists of seven key areas of learning deemed essential for a child's development in the Early Years. The childcare provider will cover each of the seven areas.

Since September 2021, early childhood settings have been using a revised EYFS, as outlined by the DfE. New ELGs were introduced in the revised version.

Developed by the government, the EYFS (DfE, 2023) sets the standards that early childhood providers must meet in order to ensure that children learn and develop effectively, as well as remain healthy and safe. In order for children to be able to succeed in school and in life, it promotes teaching and learning so that they are 'school ready' and are equipped with a broad range of knowledge and skills that allow them to achieve their full potential, as follows.

COMMUNICATION AND LANGUAGE

ELGs:

- *Listening*: To listen during larger and smaller group discussions, clarify their understanding of what they have heard with comments and questions and hold back and forth conversations.
- *Speaking*: To express their ideas, feelings and explanations, using new vocabulary, different tenses.

PHYSICAL DEVELOPMENT

ELGs:

- *Gross motor skills*: Develop balance, coordination and the ability to negotiate obstacles and use their strength in a controlled way, plus to confidently use movements like running, jumping, hopping and skipping.
- *Fine motor skills*: To properly hold and use a pencil, plus other small tools like pens, paintbrushes, knives, forks, spoons, scissors, etc.

PERSONAL SOCIAL AND EMOTIONAL DEVELOPMENT

ELGs:

- *Self-regulation*: Learn to recognise their own and others' feelings and how best to respond, learn to follow instructions and control their impulses and behaviour.
- *Managing self*: Building independence and perseverance, understanding right and wrong and that rules are there for a reason; learning about personal hygiene and healthy habits.
- *Building relationships*: To cooperate with others and be sensitive to each other's needs; to form positive relationships and friendships.

LITERACY

ELGs:

- *Comprehension*: Show that they understand stories being read to them by retelling and discussing the story in their own words; confidently use vocabulary they have learned in stories, rhymes, poems, etc.
- *Word reading*: Be able to say a sound for every letter of the alphabet (such as 'puh' for P) and some digraphs (such as 'thuh' for th), read some words using this skill.
- *Writing*: Write letters and some simple words and sentences.

MATHEMATICS

ELGs:

- *Number*: Understand how to say and write 1–10 in order, be able to recognise 1, 2, 3, 4 or 5 objects without counting, know number bonds up to 10.
- *Numerical patterns*: Count past 20, explore and compare patterns and quantities in numbers up to 10.

UNDERSTANDING THE WORLD

ELGs:

- *Past and present*: Learn about and discuss others' lives and roles in the community and society; learn about the past and compare how things were then to now.
- *People, culture and communities*: Describe their own environment and culture and be able to compare it with those in other cultures, faiths and countries.
- *The natural world*: Explore the natural world and understand what is natural and what is man-made; understand changing seasons and weather and the effects they have.

EXPRESSIVE ARTS AND DESIGN

ELGs:

- *Creating with materials*: Explore different materials, textures and techniques for creating art and explain their process; use props effectively in roleplaying and storytelling.
- *Being imaginative and expressive*: Create and tell stories of their own, sing nursery rhymes and songs from memory.

THE EARLY YEARS CURRICULUM ACROSS THE UK

ENGLAND

In England, the EYFS Statutory Framework applies to the provision of Early Years education for children between the ages of birth and five.

SCOTLAND

Pre-Birth to Three: Positive Outcomes for Scotland's Children and Families (Smarter Scotland, 2010) addresses the pre-birth to three age group.

Curriculum for Excellence (Education Scotland, n.d.) is offered to children between the ages of three and six.

In addition to the national practice guidance for Early Years in Scotland, *Realising the Ambition, Being Me* (Education Scotland, 2021) also provides a useful list of other resources.

WALES

As part of the Curriculum for Wales, the following are included:

- *Curriculum for Non-maintained Funded Settings* (Education Wales, 2022);
- *Early Childhood Play, Learning and Care in Wales* (Education Wales, 2023) for birth to five-year-olds in Wales, for childcare, play settings and schools.

NORTHERN IRELAND

The *Curricular Guidance for Pre-school Education* (CEA Rewarding Learning, 2019) covers preschool settings, and the Foundation Stage curriculum covers children aged four to six in schools.

NON-STATUTORY GUIDANCE FOR THE EYFS

In England there are many non-statutory guidance documents that can be used to support the teaching and learning of the EYFS Statutory Framework.

Development Matters (DfE, 2021) was commissioned by the government and written by a headteacher. There was a second non-statutory EYFS guidance written because of the need for a more rigorous approach to development for children from birth to five years, with a focus on learning and child development.

As a group of major Early Years sector organisations, the Early Years Coalition created *Birth to 5 Matters* (2021). This document provides an alternative guide to implementing the EYFS. As a continuation of the earlier *Development Matters* (Early Education, 2012), *Birth to 5 Matters* uses a similar format to that used in the original publication. In addition to providing detailed information on child development and Early Years practice, the guide also provides information on self-regulation, attachment and developing high-quality programmes.

Both documents are non-statutory. The DfE and Ofsted have made it clear that practitioners are not required to refer to any non-statutory guidance.

To meet the learning and development requirements set forth in the Statutory Framework (DfE, 2024), each individual setting is free to choose to use either, both, or neither of these guidelines. Reflect back to Chapter 1, which explores other non-statutory guidance including the *Oxford International Curriculum for Early Years* (OUP, 2022) and *Realising the Ambition* (Education Scotland, 2021).

CHARACTERISTICS OF EFFECTIVE (TEACHING) AND LEARNING

A discussion of the characteristics of effective teaching and learning (CoETL) is included within the EYFS Statutory Framework for group and school-based settings, as well as the non-statutory guidance documents, *Development Matters* (DfE, 2021) and *Birth to 5 Matters* (Early Years Coalition, 2021). In contrast, *Birth to 5 Matters* has removed the teaching component from its focus in recognition that the characteristics are dispositions that the child develops.

The CoETL are split into three main areas:

- playing and exploring;
- active learning;
- thinking and creating a critical lens.

Developing these characteristics over time contributes to children's engagement, enjoyment and use of their learning time.

CoETLs are essentially skills that, when developed at an early age, enable children to draw on them throughout their learning journeys. Consequently, you will find numerous examples of effective teaching and learning that can be used to enrich the teaching and learning process.

In the EYFS (DfE, 2024), the characteristics of effective teaching and learning are referred to as statutory requirements.

Overarching principles suggest:

Four guiding principles should shape practice in early years settings. These are:

- every child is a unique child, who is constantly learning and can be resilient, capable, confident and self-assured;
- children learn to be strong and independent through positive relationships;
- children learn and develop well in enabling environments, in which their experiences respond to their individual needs and there is a strong partnership between practitioners and parents and/or carers; and
- children develop and learn in different ways and at different rates. The framework covers the education and care of all children in early years provision, including children with special educational needs and disabilities. (p. 6)

They are also referred to in section 2.8:

> Year 1 teachers must be given a copy of the Profile report together with a short commentary on each child's skills and abilities in relation to the three key characteristics of effective learning (see paragraph 1.10). These should inform a dialogue between Reception and Year 1 teachers about each child's stage of development and learning needs and assist with the planning of activities in Year 1.
>
> (DfE, 2024, p. 14)

Characteristics of effective learning describe how children learn. When a child approaches opportunities with curiosity, energy and enthusiasm, they will be able to learn well. It is imperative that effective learning is meaningful to a child, so that they can apply what they have learned to new situations. As a result of these abilities and attitudes, strong learners will be able to make satisfactory progress in all areas of learning and development (Early Years Coalition, 2021).

MOVING FORWARDS: THE GENERAL DEBATE

There appears to be a firmly established school readiness agenda in the Early Years curriculum. It has been argued by Moss (2013) that society has shifted to education as a means of boosting mobility geared towards economic success, with an emphasis on preparing children for the first stage of that journey through early childhood education. Using the example of 'putting a baby in an adult suit', Ruth Swailes explores this concept. Why would you do such a thing? The young boy will wear a suit when he is older, so why not teach him now while he is still a baby? This is what we are seeing in our schools and settings today. It is what they need to learn for Key Stage 1, so we need to start them at an early age. The child will not be able to move, develop and focus on being a child due to this restriction. This is where the learning rhetoric is heading, rather than focusing on play and realising that children need opportunities to learn through an age-appropriate curriculum. In response, the EYFS framework can be interpreted as a prescriptive and homogeneous national curriculum (Palaiologou, 2016). Through the EYFS and non-statutory guidance documents such as *Development Matters in the Early Years Foundation Stage* (Early Education, 2012), the English Early Years curriculum can be positioned within a 'landscape of possibilities' (Stewart, 2016). This is positive as we know that *Birth to 5 Matters* (Early Years Coalition, 2021) was founded on the principles of the *Development Matters* (Early Education, 2012).

Birth to 5 Matters (Early Years Coalition, 2021) and the *Oxford International Curriculum for Early Years* (OUP, 2022) allow us to deliver a meaningful learning experience and child-centred approach to our children, relying on observation and interpretation embedded in participatory practices, with practitioners continuously evaluating and reviewing the curriculum's impact.

We want to envisage a pedagogy which follows a curriculum that supports children's experience of agency, belonging and membership – early childhood education should emphasise pedagogies of cooperation and participatory learning.

KEY POINTS OF THE CHAPTER

There is a clear recognition that contemporary research discussing the child as capable and competent, able to construct their own meaning and to engage with an effective curriculum through collaborative and participatory processes is an important aspect of developing a curriculum and pedagogy. We both truly feel that at the core of any curriculum or pedagogical approach there must be a centralised aspect focusing on the child, their uniqueness and the ability to adopt such an approach of teaching and learning focusing on play.

We wanted to highlight the need for a child-centred curriculum, and we know that there are many different guidances for you to use as an Early Years professional. We feel that *Birth to 5 Matters* (Early Years Coalition, 2021) would be our go-to guidance as it sits closely with our values and approaches to a child-centred EYFS.

There is a need to take stock of what is important for children. We can continue to move forwards with an agenda which places school readiness as the prime priority, or we can look at the evidence of what really matters. This is mirrored in the work of Professors Chris Pascal and Tony Bertram who were commissioned to conduct a literature review of the most recent research related to the EYFS by a group of 12 Early Years sector organisations: *Getting it Right in the Early Years Foundation Stage: A Review* (Pascal et al., 2019).

Our final note: We would like to emphasise that every child develops in a unique manner, and that development is not a linear or automatic process. Children must be provided with opportunities to interact in positive relationships and environments that encourage their engagement and recognise their strengths to develop their potential. It is important to remember that all children have agency and curiosity to learn, and that they will interact with other people and the world around them in a variety of ways. To understand who children are and how best to support their development, it is essential to understand their diverse ways of knowing about the world.

REFERENCES

Barnett, L. and Owens, M. (2015) Does play have to be playful? In J. Johnson, S. Eberle, T. Henricks and D. Kuschner, *The Handbook of the Study of Play* (pp. 453–459). Lanham, MD: Rowan & Littlefield.

Bottrill, G. (2018) *Can I Go and Play Now?* London: Sage.

CEA Rewarding Learning (2019) *Curricular Guidance for Pre-school Education*. Available at: https://ccea.org.uk/downloads/docs/ccea-asset/Curriculum/Curricular%20Guidance%20for%20Pre-School%20Education.pdf [Accessed 30 May 2024].

Center on the Developing Child (2021) *Brain Building Through Play: Activities for Infants, Toddlers, and Children*. Available at: https://developingchild.harvard.edu/resources/brain-buildingthroughplay/ [Accessed 2 February 2024].

Department for Education (DfE) (2021) *Development Matters: Non-Statutory Curriculum Guidance for the Early Years Foundation Stage*. Available at: https://assets.publishing.service.gov.uk/media/64e6002a20ae890014f26cbc/DfE_Development_Matters_Report_Sep2023.pdf [Accessed 1 January 2024].

DfE (2024) *Early Years Foundation Stage (EYFS) Statutory Framework*. Available at: www.gov.uk/government/publications/early-years-foundation-stage-framework--2 [Accessed 1 January 2024].

Dubiel, J. (2020) *Jan Dubiel on Building a Meaningful Curriculum for Every Child: Famly*. Available at: www.famly.co/blog/jan-dubiel-meaningful-curriculum-eyfs-interview [Accessed 1 January 2024].

Early Education (2012) *Development Matters in the Early Years Foundation Stage (EYFS)*. Available at: https://dera.ioe.ac.uk/id/eprint/14042/7/development%20matters%20in%20the%20early%20years%20foundation%20stage_Redacted.pdf [Accessed 1 January 2024].

Early Education (2022) *Early Years Pedagogy*. Available at: https://early-education.org.uk/early-years-pedagogy/ [Accessed 30 May 2024].

Early Years Coalition (2021) *Birth to 5 Matters Non-statutory Guidance to the Early Years Foundation Stage*. Available at: https://birthto5matters.org.uk/wp-content/uploads/2021/03/Birthto5Matters-download.pdf [Accessed 1 January 2024].

Eberle, S.G. (2014) The elements of play: Toward a philosophy and definition of play *American Journal of Play*, *6*(2), 214–233.

Education Scotland (n.d.) *Curriculum for Excellence*. Available at: https://education.gov.scot/curriculum-for-excellence/ [Accessed 30 May 2024].

Education Scotland (2021) *Realising the Ambition, Being Me: National Practice Guidance for Early Years in Scotland*. Available at: https://education.gov.scot/media/3bjpr3wa/realisingtheambition.pdf [Accessed 30 May 2024].

Education Wales (2022) *Curriculum for Non-maintained Funded Settings*. Available at: https://hwb.gov.wales/api/storage/b1801d78-38c3-4320-9818-d9996c21aef8/220914-a-curriculum-for-funded-non-maintained-nursery-settings.pdf [Accessed 30 May 2024].

Education Wales (2023) *Early Childhood Play, Learning and Care in Wales*. Available at: https://hwb.gov.wales/curriculum-for-wales/early-childhood-play-learning-and-care-in-wales [Accessed 30 May 2024].

Gray, P. (2016) Children's natural ways of learning still work: Even for the three Rs. In D.C. Geary and D.B. Berch, *Evolutionary Perspectives on Child Development and Education* (pp. 63–93). New York: Springer.

McInnes, K., Howard, J., Crowley, K. and Miles, G. (2013) The nature of adult–child interaction in the Early Years classroom: Implications for children's perceptions of play and subsequent learning behaviour. *European Early Childhood Education Research Journal, 21*(2), 268–282.

Moss, P. (2013) Beyond the investment narrative. *Contemporary Issues in Early Childhood, 14*(4), 370–372.

Ofsted (2021) *Early Years Inspection Handbook*. Available at: www.gov.uk/government/publications/early-years-inspection-handbook-eif [Accessed 1 January 2024].

Oxford University Press (OUP) (2022) *Oxford International Curriculum for Early Years: A Play-based, Student-focused Curriculum that Puts the Child at the Centre*. Available at: https://global.oup.com/education/primary/curricula/oxford-international-curriculum/early-years/?region=uk [Accessed 1 January 2024].

Pascal, C., Bertram, T. and Rouse, L. (2019) *Getting it Right in the Early Years Foundation Stage: A Review*. Early Education. Available at: www.early-education.org.uk/getting-it-right-early-years-foundation-stage-review-evidence [Accessed 1 January 2024].

Palaiologou, L. (2016) *Child Observation: A Guide for Students of Early Childhood* (3rd edn). London: Learning Matters.

Siraj-Blatchford, I., Sylva, K., Muttock, S., Gilden, R. and Bell, D. (2002) *Researching Effective Pedagogy in the Early Years. Institute of Education*. University of London. Available at: https://dera.ioe.ac.uk/id/eprint/4650/1/RR356.pdf [Accessed 1 January 2024].

Smarter Scotland (2010) *Pre-Birth to Three: Positive Outcomes for Scotland's Children and Families*. Edinburgh: Learning and Teaching Scotland.

Stewart, N. (2016) *Development Matters: A landscape of possibilities, not a roadmap*. Available at: https://eyfs.info/articles.html/teaching-and-learning/development-matters-a-landscape-of-possibilities-not-a-roadmap-r205/ [Accessed 25 March 2024].

Tovey, H. (2020) *A Froebelian Approach: Froebel's Principles and Practice Today*. Froebel Trust. Available at: www.froebel.org.uk/uploads/documents/FT-Froebels-principles-and-practice-today.pdf [Accessed 1 January 2024].

United Nations (UN) (2013) General comment no. 14 (2013) on the right of the child to have his or her best interests taken as primary consideration (art. 3, para. 1). UN Committee on the Rights of the Child. Available at: https://digitallibrary.un.org/record/778523?ln=en [Accessed 1 January 2024].

Welsh Government (2015) *Curriculum for Wales: Foundation Phase Framework*. Available at: https://hwb.gov.wales/storage/d5d8e39c-b534-40cb-a3f5-7e2e126d8077/foundation-phase-framework.pdf [Accessed 13 June 2024].

12

THE EARLY YEARS ENVIRONMENT

> *The environment plays a central role in the process of making learning meaningful. So important was this notion, that Malaguzzi defined the environment as the third teacher.*
>
> Gandini, 2011

INTRODUCTION

Since the Early Years Foundation Stage in 2009 identified the learning environment as one of its four overarching principles (the other three being the unique child, positive relationships and learning and developing in different ways and at different rates, amended to learning at different rates in the 2018 reforms), the English education system has formally acknowledged the importance of learning environments in supporting young children's learning and developing their understanding of the world in which they live and their place in it. But the idea of the importance of the environment in supporting children's learning can be traced much further back in time.

Many of the well-known theorists who helped to shape our current Early Years practice acknowledged that the environment children spend their time in impacts on their ability to succeed and thrive.

While some theorists focused on the physical environment that children spend their time in, most also acknowledged that social and emotional environments have a significant impact on children's learning. For example, Vygotsky argued that learning takes place within the social and cultural milieu, and Bronfenbrenner highlighted the dynamic relationships between children and their immediate and wider environments and social interactions in his ecological theory (1979).

One of the pioneers of nursery education in England, Margaret McMillan, argued in the early 20th century (2009/1914) that children from one to seven years of age need space to be able to run, explore and develop their self-control as a key determinant to physical development.

Even further back, Maria Montessori pioneered the idea that an environment can be designed specifically to facilitate independent learning in children. If we go as far back as the early 19th century, Friedrich Froebel identified that the environment and atmosphere are as important to children's learning as what they actually learn.

Loris Malaguzzi, founder of the Reggio Emilia movement, argued

> the classroom environment can help shape a child's identity as a powerful player in their own life and the lives of others. To foster such an environment, teachers must go deeper than what is merely seen at eye level and develop a deep understanding of the underlying principles and of children's thinking, questions, and curiosities.
>
> (Elkind, 2018)

Thus, we can see that the idea of the learning environment as a valuable tool in children's learning has a long and rich history. This is no coincidence. Theorists and staff working with young children acknowledge that the environment can make a huge difference to young children's early development.

WHY IS IT IMPORTANT?

It is often helpful when discussing the impact of learning environments to reflect on this from a personal perspective. Imagine you are starting a new job. What do you need to be successful? You probably need to know that you have the right equipment and resources to do your job properly. Is there enough space for you to be able to work effectively? Do you have the right tools? Are the routines and expectations clear? Is this a safe space where mistakes can be rectified and different needs are accommodated and supported? If we consider the things that give us anxiety when we start a new role, it can help us reflect on what children might feel like when they enter our learning environments for the first time.

Where do I put my belongings? Is there a space for me? What's the routine? How will I know what to do? What are the expectations? What happens if I get something wrong?

All of these are natural anxieties and if we don't address them, we as adults can't function at our best. This is no different for children.

An effective learning environment needs to provide children with the tools, resources and equipment they need to be successful, but also with the emotional support and agency they need to be willing to have a go, to make mistakes, to persevere and to explore different ways of doing things. In short, to develop the CoETL which will set them up to be lifelong learners. These characteristics – engagement, motivation and creating and thinking critically – are a vital part of our statutory curriculum and research evidence suggests that children who demonstrate strong CoETL are significantly more likely to achieve well, not just in the Foundation Stage but well beyond and into adulthood (McClelland et al., 2013).

We know an enabling and effective learning environment allows us to support the development of these characteristics, so what do we need to consider when building our own learning environments?

Both the EPPE and subsequent REPEY studies acknowledge the importance of effective learning environments but the REPEY study highlights that the environment alone will not teach the children.

Malaguzzi's 'third teacher' is a flexible environment, where teachers and children create learning together. This is often referred to as 'sustained, shared thinking' (Siraj-Blatchford et al., 2019). Everything about our environment reflects the values we want to communicate to children. We often talk about 'enabling environments' as though there is an agreed definition of what this should look like. Working with schools and settings I am frequently asked about classroom layouts, essential items and areas of learning. But an enabling environment will differ according to the needs of the children and their ages and stages of development. It is beneficial to start with some thoughts on the purpose of an enabling environment.

WHAT'S THE PURPOSE?

Our environment should support and enhance children's learning and develop the skills they need to become curious, independent and motivated learners. To experiment and explore, to share and take turns and work together, develop the CoETL and to deepen their understanding of all areas of the curriculum.

HOW MIGHT THIS LOOK IN PRACTICE?

Resources should be provided that the children can use independently, that they can access without having to ask an adult and which they can care for and put back in the right place so that everyone can find them when they need them. There are many ways to ensure that environments are accessible to children. Open-ended shelving, taking the doors off cupboards to show what is behind them, clear storage boxes or reducing the number of trays in a storage unit are all ways to make resources easier for children to see. It is helpful to get down to the level of the children you're working with in order to see what the learning environment looks like from their perspective. Can they see what's available?

It's also helpful to think about ways in which you can support children to keep areas tidy by putting resources back in the right places when they have finished with them. Too many resources can feel overwhelming for children and can make selection and replacing tricky. Resources should be chosen with care, with everything earning its place. The use of photographs to show 'what tidy looks like' can support children to leave an area as they found it. Some settings also choose to use 'match-back' or 'shadowing' of resources to show where the resources go. This can help children to see where to return objects and also builds their observational skills. Young children enjoy being independent and this builds their personal, social and emotional skills. It is tempting to provide many resources at once for young children, but this can sometimes lead to a feeling of overwhelm with too many things to put away and too many things to choose from. It can also mean that for children who don't want to share, take turns or engage with others, they don't always have to do so. Sometimes when there are too many resources children can also move quickly from one thing to another, so it can be helpful to reduce what's available, particularly when settling in, so that adults can model and children learn what the resources can do and have the opportunity to reuse familiar resources. When children revisit a familiar resource they often take their ideas and fascinations further as they become more adept at using the resource and understand its properties and possibilities. It is important to show children how resources can be used, and to reinforce expectations. I use the phrase, 'choose it, use it, put it away' with the children and have found that with repetition and reinforcement and the right visual supports even the very young can tidy up after themselves.

By allowing the children to be independent we reduce their dependence on adults for 'secretarial' tasks such as fetching and putting things away. This allows the adults to focus on their interactions with the children. These early interactions, the serve and return of conversation from an early age, have been shown to change children's early brain architecture and help form neuronal connections (Golinkoff and Hirsh-Pasek, 2016) and are vital for children's early development.

WHAT DOES AN ENABLING ENVIRONMENT LOOK LIKE?

Having clearly defined spaces or areas can help children to see where resources go, and to consider what might happen in each area of learning. Using furniture to create zones can also help to naturally limit the size of a group of children in an area, which can help those who might feel overwhelmed in a larger group. Furniture can be used to create a feeling of enclosure, which young children often seek out. It's important that the furniture allows adults a clear view of all areas of the classroom, while providing a cosy space for the children.

If at all possible, furniture should be low height so children can access it and see what's on the surfaces, which can be used to display resources or as a place to keep 'work in progress'. High units can feel oppressive to small children, will limit sight lines and can lead to children trying to reach for things above their height which could be dangerous. Choose furniture wisely. Sometimes the furniture in a space is less than ideal; if you're in a setting and want a particular type of furniture, it's always helpful to check storage to see if there are items hidden away, or to place a photograph of the type of furniture you want on a noticeboard; someone may have the exact item you want in another part of the building and be willing to swap for an item that's more suitable for their needs.

CONTINUOUS PROVISION: HOW MUCH SHOULD CHANGE AND WHEN?

This is a topic that comes up for discussion frequently. Many people feel that provision should be changed because children might get bored having the same tools and resources all the time, but this is rarely the case. Sometimes people make changes because others perceive that having the same resources available all the time shows a lack of thought from the practitioners. I do not subscribe to these views. If we reflect on the purpose of an enabling environment – to develop key skills and allow children to become proficient with tools and resources and develop their independence – constantly changing resources can be counterproductive. If adults have chosen resources thoughtfully and carefully children should be able to use them repeatedly and in a multitude of ways. By allowing children to revisit these resources their skills develop over time and their skills and thinking can often become much deeper than their initial play. Children need opportunities to revise and revisit prior learning and provision allows them opportunities to do so in a safe and familiar environment. It may be that from time to time staff will choose to add an enhancement or a provocation to an area of the provision, to deepen thinking, to allow for a particular skill that has been taught to be developed or maybe to introduce a new concept or skill, but there is no need to provide enhancements in every area of the provision. In my experience working in and with settings for the last three decades, too many enhancements that change too often can lead to children moving quickly from one area to another; if they are not sure how long the enhancement will remain in place there can be a desire to experience everything quickly in case it disappears. This doesn't lead to deep thinking and learning and can also mean that adults have to intervene in several areas of the provision to ensure that children are using the enhancements as intended. This is counterproductive, reduces independence skills and impacts negatively on the interactions staff can have with the children. As with all resources, enhancements should earn their place too. A good question to ask is, 'Is what I'm putting out as an enhancement better than what the children would do independently with the provision?' If the answer is no, it's probably best not to bother with the enhancement. The Statutory Framework mentions that children should make choices about how they learn. An enhancement in every area of provision effectively removes that choice from the child and hands it back to the member of staff. It sends a message that provision on its own is not good enough and removes the child's agency from their learning. Albert Bandura (2012) defined self-efficacy as people's belief in their ability to control their functioning and events that affect their lives and recognised that one's sense of self-efficacy can provide the foundation for motivation, wellbeing and personal accomplishment. Stewart (2013) links those with a strong sense of self-efficacy to the CoETL.

We have an innate need to be/feel effective self-efficacy; those with a strong sense of self-efficacy show many of the characteristics of effective learners:

- they approach challenges as something to be mastered;
- they develop deep interest and commitment to their activities; and
- they bounce back from setbacks.

We should bear this in mind when providing enhancements.

WHAT AREAS OF LEARNING DO I NEED?

This is one of the most frequently asked questions when building an enabling environment. It's useful to consider your current priorities: what do the children need most support with and which areas would facilitate such learning? Which areas of the current learning environment do children enjoy visiting the most? Where do you hear the most discussion? Which areas provide the richest learning opportunities? It's also important to consider space and resourcing. There are very few settings where it's possible to have every single area of provision; space and resourcing are often key factors in making these decisions. For example, it would be lovely to have a large sand area that children can step into in the outdoor area, but if space and resourcing do not allow, there's no point in making this a priority unless you have the funding to do so. There are no 'statutory' areas in an Early Years learning environment. What you choose to provide is based on your children's needs and interests, your key priorities, current resources, time and space.

It's worth considering how you would make a case for an area of provision if you were to have to 'sell' it to someone.

Let's take the sand area as an example. In most Early Years settings sand is provided because many children enjoy playing with the sand. It also provides a range of opportunities to develop many areas of learning.

THE CASE FOR SAND

Sand provides children with a broad range of rich and meaningful experiences. Depending on their age and stage of development children will use sand in a variety of ways. Very young children enjoy the sensory experience of feeling sand slip through their fingers and are often fascinated to watch sand fall as it is poured out of buckets; older children will often create quite complex storytelling scenarios and use their problem-solving and reasoning skills as well as developing manipulative and play skills.

WHAT CONCEPTS MIGHT BE DEVELOPED HERE?

Sand can provide an introduction to many scientific concepts such as gravity, absorption and reversible changes, mathematical concepts such as volume and capacity, empty and full, as well as creative opportunities to build worlds using wet sand. Young children will enjoy sensory play in sand, and adding water to form different consistencies can be the stimulus for interesting discussions. There are many opportunities to develop children's PSED skills, ensuring they are mindful of others when playing in the sand, becoming aware of and managing risk, sharing and taking turns. Sand is often a place where observational and parallel play takes place and children may progress to associative and cooperative play. Sand provides opportunities to develop early language and communication from commenting with very young children 'It's sticky', to developing more subject-specific vocabulary. Sand also provides opportunities to develop core strength and shoulder-girdle strength when lifting heavy buckets and fine motor control when manipulating tools.

WHAT CONVERSATIONS MIGHT I HAVE HERE TO SUPPORT LEARNING? WHAT COMMENTS MIGHT I MAKE?

Commenting on what you notice or feel can be very helpful when developing young children's language. Describing what you see, 'It feels scratchy' or 'It's cold', can help young children develop their own vocabulary. As children become more confident, pose simple questions, 'I wonder what would happen if …?' or make comments, 'That's interesting, the water seems to have disappeared', to stimulate discussions. Sand can be an ideal place to introduce comparative mathematical vocabulary such as empty, full, heavier, lighter. It also lends itself to prepositions, 'Can you put your sandcastle next to mine? Let's make another one behind it.'

THINGS TO CONSIDER

For a larger space, a 'sit in' sand pit at ground level is ideal and will provide a full, sensory immersive experience. Think about how you will protect it from elements and animals. In a smaller space, a sand tray will suffice. Think about how much space there is and choose resources accordingly. Too many resources in a small sand tray may impact negatively on the quality of play. Too few in a large pit might lead to children playing in isolation. Think about what resources children need, they will naturally enjoy pouring, filling and emptying containers; they will also want to use containers as moulds in wet sand. It is helpful to have a range of tools to shape the sand. Consider what resources children might need if they are to use the sand for storying opportunities. Ensure that they can carefully select any resources and that it's clear where they need to return them to when they have finished. Don't forget to teach children about the dangers of throwing and of eating sand. The properties of wet and dry sand are very different; add water from time to time to ensure that children experience the different properties.

THE 5CS APPROACH

This 5Cs approach: *case, concepts, comments and conversations, considerations* can enable everyone involved with developing the learning environment to really reflect on the core purpose of an area of learning.

Organising the learning environment can feel quite overwhelming. It helps to break it down into different areas of learning and tackle one part at a time. It is also important to remember that the learning environment outdoors is of equal importance and can provide opportunities that are not always available indoors. Depending on the space available, outdoors can be larger, louder and more physically demanding. However, practitioners should not lose sight of the purpose of the learning environment; they should ask the same questions when developing indoors as outdoors and using the 5Cs approach can help. Think carefully about every area in the provision earning its place and every resource being purposeful. Organising outdoors can be challenging, especially in pack-away settings or for those sharing a space with others. Many settings struggle with setting up when this is the place that parents walk through to drop off and collect children; often younger siblings are tempted to play with resources and this can mean that the provision isn't always set out as staff would like. One way to overcome this is by setting up storage solutions. Outdoor storage sheds come in all shapes and sizes and some are reasonably priced, particularly the heavy plastic type which are designed to house garden tools, etc. By placing shelving inside these units and setting them up in a similar way to indoor provision, with photographs to support tidying, the same principles can be used in the indoor environment as the outdoor environment.

REFLECTION POINTS

- Which parts of your environment currently work really well?
- Why might that be?
- Which area are you going to reflect on and develop using the 5Cs?

KEY POINTS OF THE CHAPTER

- The learning environment can be a powerful tool for teaching many key skills.
- Everything in the environment should earn its place.
- Breaking the environment down into different spaces helps to make the task of developing an enabling environment manageable.
- The 5Cs approach can help everyone to understand the purpose of the learning environment.
- Enhancements should be used judiciously.
- The environment should build children's knowledge, skills and CoETL.
- The environment should enable staff to have high-quality interactions with the children.
- The environment is both a physical and emotional space; interactions are as important, if not more so, than the resources in the environment.

REFERENCES

Bandura, A. (2012) *Self-efficacy: The Exercise of Control*. New York: W.H. Freeman.

Bronfenbrenner, U. (1979) *The Ecology of Human Development: Experiments by Nature and Design*. Cambridge, MA: Harvard University Press.

Elkind, D. (2018) *The Power of Play: Learning What Comes Naturally*. Vancouver, BC: Langara College.

Gandini, L. (2011) *Play and the Hundred Languages of Children: An Interview with Lella Gandini*. Dordrecht: Education Linguistics.

Golinkoff, R.M. and Hirsh-Pasek, K. (2016) *Becoming Brilliant: What Science Tells Us About Raising Successful Children*. Washington, DC: American Psychological Association.

McClelland, M.M., Acock, A.C., Piccinin, A., Rhea, S.A. and Stallings, M.C. (2013) Relations between preschool attention span-persistence and age 25 educational outcomes. *Early Childhood Research Quarterly*, 28(2), 314–324. doi:10.1016/j.ecresq.2012.07.008.

McMillan, M. (2009/1914) *The Nursery School*. Charleston, SC: BiblioLife.

Siraj, I., Kingston, D. and Neilsen-Hewett, C. (2019) The role of professional development in improving quality and supporting child outcomes in early education and care. *Pacific Early Childhood Education Research Association*, 13, 49–68.

Stewart, N. (2013) Active Learning. In H. Moylett, *Characteristics of Effective Learning: Helping Young Children Become Learners for Life* (1st edn) (pp. 54–71). Maidenhead: Open University Press.

13

EQUALITY, DIVERSITY AND INCLUSION

> *A commitment to valuing and respecting the diversity of individuals, families and communities must sit at the heart of early years practice. Inequalities persist in society, with far-reaching effects on children's education, health and life chances.*
>
> Early Years Coalition, 2021, p. 24

INTRODUCTION

The principles of inclusion and equality apply to all children and families. In order to attain equality, we must consider practices from the perspective of all individuals and groups, not just those from minoritised groups. Taking part in community practices builds a child's identity, values and a family's unique knowledge over the course of time.

This chapter looks at the EYFS and how we can become more aligned to the focus of equality, diversity and inclusion. A variety of early childhood settings provide the opportunity for children and their families to thrive and achieve their full potential in a diverse, equal and inclusive environment. One of the 17 Sustainable Development Goals (SDGs) of the United Nations (n.d.) is to 'ensure inclusive and equitable quality education and to promote lifelong learning opportunities for all'. In the context of early childhood education, what are the meanings of equality, diversity, and inclusion (EDI)? This chapter is going to give you a brief overview of what EDI looks and should feel like in the EYFS.

Birth to 5 Matters' EYFS guidance (Early Years Coalition, 2021) emphasises the importance of inclusion and equality for all children and their families. It is important to recognise, discuss and value racial and cultural differences in addition to treating everyone equally. The environment should reflect the experiences of the children so that they can develop a sense of belonging. It is the view of special education needs (SEN) practitioners that disabilities are seen from a strengths-based perspective, emphasising what a child is capable of achieving. A child should always be the centre of attention in any picture.

Our day-to-day role requires us to practise inclusive practices and promote equality. An individual's diversity must be valued and respected. Children, families and the whole community must be at the centre of early childhood practices. It is impossible to ignore the inequalities within society that have a detrimental effect on children's development, education, health and future prospects. It is important for settings to explicitly address all forms of discrimination and prejudice as stated in the *Birth to 5 Matters* guidance (Early Years Coalition, 2021, p. 24).

As a professional, you can accomplish this within the context of the setting and follow the Equality Act 2010 and its requirement that no child or family be discriminated against on the basis of their protected characteristics, as illustrated in Figure 13.1.

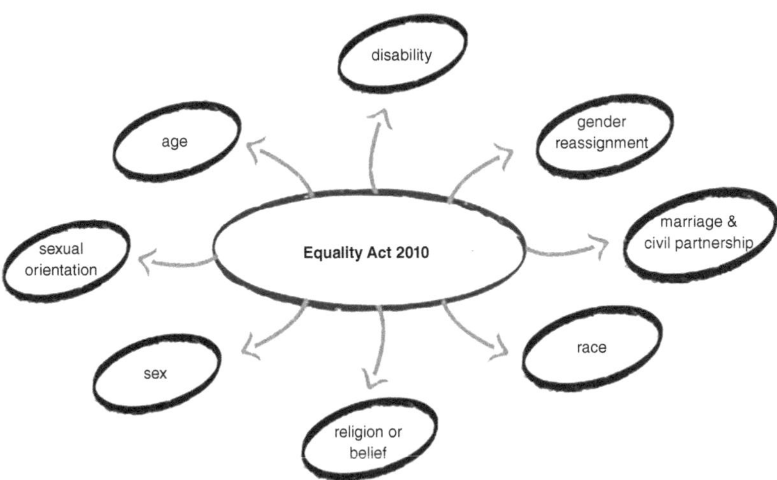

Figure 13.1 Equality Act 2010

Birth to 5 Matters (Early Years Coalition, 2021) explains that the practice of early childhood education must place a strong emphasis on valuing and respecting the diversity of individuals, families and communities. Children's education, health and life chances are adversely affected by persistent inequalities in society. In order to effectively address all forms of discrimination and prejudice, early childhood settings have a crucial role to play.

As a result, we will be able to comply with the Equality Act 2010 requirement that no child or family is discriminated against on the basis of the following protected characteristics: age, disability, gender reassignment, race, religion or belief, sex, sexual orientation, marriage and civil partnership (Early Years Coalition, 2021).

THE UNIQUE CHILD

We wanted to focus on why it is important to understand what we mean by the unique child. Each child develops at their own pace and is unique. As part of the Early Years Foundation Stage, this is an overarching principle.

> Every child is a unique child, who is constantly learning and can be resilient, capable, confident and self-assured.
>
> (Early Years Coalition, 2021, p. 8)

The basics of inclusive practice is to understand each child as unique in their own way. As *Birth to 5 Matters* puts it:

> Identifying what each unique child 'knows and can do' is the foundation of inclusive early years practice.
>
> (Early Years Coalition, 2021, p. 9)

Since this is what is required as a minimum standard, not only do we need to identify what each child can do, but also we need to know and understand what their learning interests are during every stage of their development, and especially during each moment we spend with them. A schematic play approach can be extremely beneficial in assessing the unique characteristics of each child.

The philosophy underpinning the new EYFS encourages the child to be unique and individual, as long as they meet the age and stage requirements for the four themes:

- a unique child;
- positive relationships;
- enabling environments;
- children develop and learn at different rates.

Even though we recognise the constructive nature of this approach, the delineation of what is required has remained unchanged since 2008. According to the original spirit of the EYFS, 'whatever children bring is an indication of their current interest and should be supported' (DCSF, 2008, p. 7).

Bradbury and Grimmer (2024) explore how a loving and nurturing environment can support the unique child. They argue that the learning environment is something that we don't always link to the unique child. The environment sets the scene for children to be able to flourish, and they believe that this is done through relationships, further discussing the importance of love and nurture. We might challenge the inclusiveness of a setting if the door is always closed, the staff rarely smile and when a child with an additional need visits the focus is on the problems rather than possible solutions. Similarly, if a setting claims to care but has little time to spend with families and does not engage in nurturing and loving interactions with the children, this ethos may be questioned.

When we consider what constitutes the unique child we believe in what Bradbury and Grimmer (2024) argue for a loving and nurturing environment. They allow us to challenge and reflect upon our core values, ethos and how these ideals are lived out through our daily Early Years practices. Some of the attributes of a loving, nurturing environment with a main focus on the unique child are:

- safe
- welcoming
- inclusive
- accessible
- emotionally enabling
- empowering
- calm and natural
- holds children in mind.

It is important to recognise that each child is unique and will flourish within an inclusive environment. In other words, we strive to ensure that every child feels included, welcome and that they belong to us. Inclusionary early childhood providers ensure that no child or family is disadvantaged as a result of background, ethnicity, language at home, religion, or disability. This does not happen automatically, but rather is achieved by ensuring our policies and practices are as inclusive as possible, as well as getting to know our children and families well. In order to support and include children, we will need to work together with their families and reflect on and meet their individual needs in partnership with them.

The use of accurate language is another aspect of being inclusive. The use of language is an emotive topic, and some individuals have strong opinions regarding how they would like to be described. Therefore, it is always recommended that you ask the individual. People with autism may wish to be called autistic or neurodiverse, or people who are gay may wish to be called queer. You can also request which pronouns should be used and add your preference to the staff list or your email signature. We would state that for children who come from families where this is their daily lives, it is important that they feel like their unique abilities are being seen and acted upon.

In order for resources to be accessible, they must reflect different cultures, abilities and local communities. How can we make the use of non-English languages part of children's everyday experiences when considering our resources? For example, can a local bakery that caters to a non-English speaking population provide us with some food packets for our home corner? Is it possible for the families who attend to share some packaging with us in order to make this area more familiar to the children if we include foods consumed at home? In particular, this is useful if the packaging is written in a language other than English.

The benefits of an inclusive environment are numerous; some are listed below:

- every child feels like they matter, are valued, loved and belong;
- children feel safe and secure;
- children have equal access to activities and resources;
- resources reflect the children, different cultures and the local community;
- provision contains various areas for quiet and noisy play, including places to rest and calm down;
- children's self-esteem is fostered and they are encouraged to be independent.

(Bradbury and Grimmer, 2024)

INCLUSION IN THE EARLY YEARS

It is important to note that everyone has their own interpretation of the term 'inclusion' and that inclusion can take different forms depending on the context. In whatever way you define it, your policies, practices, attitudes and values must combine to ensure everyone feels at home: children, parents, staff and all those associated with your institution.

Some people mistakenly believe that inclusion applies only to children who are identified as having special educational needs or disabilities and who attend non-specialist schools. Inclusion, however, is only one aspect of the topic. Aiming to be inclusive means scrutinising policies, practices, attitudes and values that shape early childhood communities in order to ensure that everyone feels safe, comfortable and welcomed. Their individuality and heritage are respected, and they are recognised for who they are. It is important for them to have their needs met and to be able to contribute.

The concept of inclusion includes understanding the individual, the family, the culture, the society, the setting and the practitioners, and working respectfully to eliminate discriminatory practices. To achieve inclusion, anti-discriminatory practices must be in place (Colilles, 2023) along with an understanding of when a practice is discriminatory. Louis et al. (2023) explain that:

> Anti-discriminatory practice is defined as a professional method of continually challenging racism, sexism, stereotypes, bias and inequalities.

> Discrimination may manifest itself in many different ways, including someone's attitude, behaviour, the curriculum and resources they provide, or their values, beliefs and ideologies.
>
> (Louis et al., 2023, p. 96)

The document *Birth to 5 Matters* reminds us of several key points in relation to inclusive practice and equalities:

- Equalities and inclusion apply to all children and families.
- Equity requires more than treating everyone the same.
- Talking about race is a first step in countering racism.
- Building awareness through first-hand experiences has lasting impact.
- Ensure children can see themselves and their families reflected in the environment.
- Focus on the child at the centre.
- Practitioners working with children with Special Educational Needs and Disabilities (SEND) acknowledge and value each child, emphasising what they can do through a strengths-based perspective on disability.

(Early Years Coalition, 2021, p. 27)

GENDER IN THE EARLY YEARS

You may assume that gender discrimination in early childhood settings has decreased as a result of changes in legislation, awareness and practices related to gender equality. Despite this, stereotyping still occurs: 'In terms of gender and sexual orientation, young children can develop stereotypical ideas about how they should be and who they should become which can limit their potential' (Early Years Coalition, 2021, p. 25).

The gender-based expectations of behaviours, academic preferences and perceived abilities may already be in place by the time children enter early learning settings. Their attitudes towards relationships, participation in the world of work, as well as their wellbeing can be impacted by these stereotypical views. In the course of life, a narrowing of experiences at this stage often leads to a narrowing of opportunities. It is important for Early Years practitioners to challenge these views before they become too engrained, despite the fact that the problem is multifaceted. It is essential that children should not be coerced into any activity, but adopting the attitude that they have the freedom to make their own choices will not solve the problem. There are many instances in which children self-select out of certain activities based upon their observation of what is appropriate in their environment.

To ensure equality of opportunity in the future, it is essential that children are given the opportunity to access all areas of the curriculum at an early age. It is the skill of early childhood practitioners to focus on the specific needs of each child and to act in a child-centred manner. There has been a turbulent landscape surrounding the representation of LGBTQ+ and gender among young children in recent years (Bradbury, 2023), which includes discussions around gender (DePalma, 2016; Parveen, 2019), which can lead to protest and strong opposition from professionals and certain parent groups. There is, however, a need for a balanced, sensitive and sympathetic approach from early childhood practitioners who can collaborate with other relevant professionals to provide support to children and parents.

A number of approaches have been described by Tembo and Benham (2023) to support gender and LGBTQ+ inclusion and to enhance children's opportunities by allowing them to express themselves and explore their own identities. This type of discussion should begin during the early years of a child's development. The early childhood profession is in a unique position to disrupt the landscape of gender normalising pedagogies and practices (Robinson and Jones-Diaz, 2006). It is possible to challenge gender stereotypes within early childhood settings and practices by creating a nurturing and sympathetic environment for later childhood and adulthood that promotes gender variation and sexual orientation (Bradbury, 2023; Luecke, 2011).

REFLECTION 13.1

TACKLING YOUR OWN UNCONSCIOUS BIAS

In our interactions with children it is important to be aware of our unconscious biases.

This influences how we interact with children differently, the assumptions we make and the advice and directions we provide. It is important to identify, reflect on and discuss your own biases openly with colleagues, regardless of how challenging it may be to admit and deal with them.

Take on board some of these questions.

Can you identify any implicit assumptions you might make about the types of activities and curriculum areas that children prefer?

Does your expectation and/or acceptance of boys' and girls' behaviour differ? For example, do you expect girls to behave more quietly and boys to behave more boisterously?

Can you encourage children to participate in activities associated with not just their own gender when they are participating in activities associated with their own gender?

ANTI-RACIST PRACTICE IN THE EARLY YEARS

Daniel (2023) argues that we need to make anti-racism a real thing in our learning environments and reflect upon and continually review provision. Daniel goes on to say that Early Years educators can ensure that they are committed to their remit of advocacy for the children and communities whose lives they touch. *Development Matters* (DFE, 2021, p. 103) states that we need to 'notice differences between people'. Further to this *Birth to 5 Matters* states that 'talking about race is a first step in countering racism' (Early Years Coalition, 2021, p. 22). We can draw upon both of these documents to help us understand why anti-racism needs to be at the forefront of our practices.

Racism can be countered by talking about race. Treating all people equally and ignoring racial differences is not a sufficient response to racism. Through this approach, the bias in society which disadvantages people from systemically marginalised groups will continue to exist.

It is important for practitioners to receive training in order to open dialogue and develop a deeper understanding of white privilege, systemic racism and how racism affects children and families in early childhood settings. It is also a time to teach children about racial equality in a way which is age and stage appropriate, but it needs to take place. It is possible for children to maintain or reinforce their racial prejudice and misconceptions when adults remain silent about race. Children's strong sense of fairness can be evoked by dialogue and conversation about difference, thus breaking down false assumptions that each individual can achieve success for themselves. This will help them recognise racist behaviour and develop a strong sense of anti-racism.

REFLECTION 13.2

WE CAN MAKE A DIFFERENCE

Bradbury and Pemberton (2020) explain that our Early Years education settings need to become clear about the national narrative. They need to reflect on real-world experiences and the child's cultural capital. We cannot just raise children's awareness of family diversity and diversity in the home as it does not go far enough.

Where do you start?

Below are some questions to help you reflect on your practice.

Are you bringing the topic of race into your setting in a way that children can understand and ask about? For example, this could be through books, pictures and stories.

Are you giving your children in your setting an accurate representation of the world?

Do you encourage questions about race when children ask about them?

Are you putting the unique child at the heart of your practices?

CONTINUOUS PROVISION

When considering equality, diversity and inclusion, we need to think about our continuous provision as EDI should permeate through it. Our ethos should make sure that the Early Years environment reflects our daily routines, and the interactions we have with children needs to reflect the needs and backgrounds of all in the setting. The term 'continuous provision' refers to the provision of quality resources both inside and outside the classroom that children are able to interact with and access on a daily basis. As part of continuous provision, children are provided with an environment that is safe for exploration while also providing a level of challenge. It is through play and discovery that children are able to gain independence and learn how to make decisions. If an adult is not present, children should be able to continue their learning in the provision.

It is crucially important to have continuous provision in order to promote active, curious learners and to allow children the opportunity to choose areas of their Early Years setting to go and follow an interest in and which they would like to explore further. Early Years practitioners can model speech and extend vocabulary during rich conversations. Children become self-confident, curious and resilient when continuous provision is valued, open-ended, skills based and well resourced.

KEY POINTS OF THE CHAPTER

The importance of reflecting on our attitudes, behaviour and practices cannot be overstated. Observations of adults around young children have a profound effect on their attitudes towards diversity. There is no alternative to inclusion. Early Years settings have legal and moral responsibilities in this area, as well as children having defined entitlements.

It is essential that we examine our own thoughts, attitudes and assumptions regarding difference and diversity in order to fulfil these responsibilities.

(Continued)

In order to overcome barriers for children, we must be aware that a number of barriers exist that are not always obvious or immediately apparent, particularly subconscious and attitude-based barriers.

To avoid successive generations of children experiencing bias and inequality that can lead to underachievement, it is imperative that we are able to examine our feelings and attitudes sensitively, honestly and openly.

Approaches to take forwards:

1. it is never too late to engage in continuous professional development;
2. reflective practice is key here;
3. developing safe spaces so that conversations, challenge and learning can take place is important;
4. resources and the environment are key to achieving an inclusive setting. Review this regularly so that the whole community is represented;
5. continually be the voices of all children, advocate for them and develop empathic practices. It is never too late to make that difference for all children.

REFERENCES

Bradbury, A. (2023) Working with LGBT+ parent led families. In P. Thompson and H. Simmons, *Partnership With Parents in Early Childhood Today* (Chapter 6). London: Learning Matters.

Bradbury, A. and Grimmer, T. (2024) *Love and Nurture in the Early Years*. London: Learning Matters.

Bradbury, A. and Pemberton, L. (FAMLY) (2020) *The Early Years Inclusion Revolution*. Available at: www.famly.co/blog/early-years-inclusion-revolution [Accessed 1 December 2023].

Colilles, S. (2023) Inclusive pedagogies. *Early Education Journal*, 99, 10–12.

Daniel, V. (2023) *Anti Racist Practice in the Early Years*. London: Routledge.

DePalma, R. (2016) Gay penguins, sissy ducklings … and beyond? Exploring gender and sexuality diversity through children's literature. *Discourse: Studies in the Cultural Politics of Education*, 37(6), 828–845.

Department for Children, Schools and Families (DCSF) (2008) *Department for Children, Schools and Families Departmental Report*. Available at: www.gov.uk/government/publications/department-for-children-schools-and-families-departmental-report-2008 [Accessed 1 November 2023].

Department for Education (DfE) (2021) *Development Matters: Non-Statutory Curriculum Guidance for the Early Years Foundation Stage*. Available at: https://assets.publishing.service.gov.uk/media/64e6002a20ae890014f26cbc/DfE_Development_Matters_Report_Sep2023.pdf [Accessed 1 January 2024].

Early Years Coalition (2021) *Birth to 5 Matters Non-statutory Guidance to the Early Years Foundation Stage*. Available at: https://birthto5matters.org.uk/wp-content/uploads/2021/03/Birthto5Matters-download.pdf [Accessed 1 January 2024].

Equality Act 2010. Available at: www.legislation.gov.uk/ukpga/2010/15/contents [Accessed 30 May 2024].

Louis, S., Cave, S. and Meah, N. (2023) Race, anti-discrimination and work to combat the effects of discrimination on practitioners and children. In C. Nutbrown, *Early Childhood Education: Current Realities and Future Priorities*. London: Sage.

Luecke, J.C. (2011) Working with transgender children and their classmates in pre-adolescence: Just be supportive. *Journal of LGBT Youth*, 8(2), 116–156.

Parveen, N. (2019) Birmingham school stops LGBT lessons after parents protest. *Guardian* (Monday, 4 March). www.theguardian.com/education/2019/mar/04/birmingham-school-stops-lgbt-lessons-after-parent-protests [Accessed 1 January 2024].

Robinson, K.H. and Jones-Diaz, C. (2006) *Diversity and Difference in Early Childhood Education: Issues for Theory and Practice*. Maidenhead: Open University Press.

Tembo, S. and Benham, F. (2023) Gender and LGBTQ+ inclusive practice in early childhood. In C. Nutbrown, *Early Childhood Education: Current Realities and Future Priorities*. London: Sage.

United Nations (UN) (n.d.) *The 17 Goals*. Available at: https://sdgs.un.org/goals [Accessed 30 May 2024].

14

CHILDREN WITH SPECIAL EDUCATIONAL NEEDS AND DISABILITIES

The statutory framework for the Early Years Foundation Stage (2024) is clear that practitioners must consider the individual needs, interests and development of each child in their care to ensure a strong foundation in their learning and development. Working in partnership with parents plays a key role in enabling all children to reach their full potential and gives practitioners an insight into the child's home context.

DfE, 2024

INTRODUCTION

Early childhood education should be of high quality for all children. We must recognise children's starting points as early childhood professionals, build on their interests and demonstrate what they are capable of. There should be equality at the core of every provision, ensuring that children, parents and other professionals all feel a sense of belonging and that their voices are heard. We should all strive to get it right and learn from our children to be able to adapt to and respond to their individual needs.

This chapter looks at how high-quality early education is important for all children, but particularly powerful for children from disadvantaged backgrounds and for children with delayed learning and development. The chapter highlights four key points of working with children with special educational needs and disabilities, including:

- law and legislation: the rights of the child;
- a voice for every child;
- Early Years curriculum;
- working with parents.

To ensure that a child's voice and rights are recognised, working with parents is crucial. Observations and observational support should take place in a reciprocal manner, where professionals observe what the child is doing and identify their needs and support needs. To address this need, professionals need to make use of their planning and provide meaningful opportunities for children to reach their full potential. Through the lens of loving pedagogy, Grimmer (2021) discusses and explores this issue. In order for children to become confident and learn within an environment, their voice must be at the forefront of our practices. For some children, implementing next steps and some differentiated interventions may be sufficient to ensure their development. The setting and experience within the Early Years can be challenging for other children. In these circumstances, professionals must be sensitive to the needs of the child in order to ensure that all children are given the opportunity to reach their full potential. Schools and Early Years settings that are registered with Ofsted are legally required to ensure that they meet the needs of children who require additional support with their learning and development. According to the *Special Educational Needs and Disability Code of Practice* (DfE and DoH, 2015) (SEND), statutory duties include identifying, assessing and making provision for children with special educational needs and/or disabilities.

LAW AND LEGISLATION: THE RIGHTS OF THE CHILD

The SEND *Code of Practice* (DfE and DoH, 2015, pp. 15–16) defines special educational needs and disability as follows:

> A child or young person has special educational needs if they have a learning difficulty or disability which calls for special educational provision to be made for him or her.
>
> A child of compulsory school age or a young person has a learning difficulty or disability if [they]:
>
> - [have] a significantly greater difficulty in learning than the majority of others of the same age, or
> - [have] a disability which prevents or hinders them from making use of facilities generally provided for others of the same age in mainstream schools.

A child should not be regarded as having a learning disability solely because the language used in their home is different from the language used in school.

According to the *Code of Practice* (DfE and DoH, 2015, p. 16), special educational provision means:

> For children aged two or more, special educational provision is educational or training provision that is additional to, or different from, that made generally for other children or young people of the same age by mainstream schools, maintained nursery schools, mainstream post-16 institutions, or by relevant early years providers.
>
> For children under age two, special educational provision means educational provision of any kind.

As outlined in the Children and Families Act (2014), the *Code of Practice* (DfE and DoH, 2015, p. 19) is based on three main principles. A clear statement is made in these regulations that local authorities must consider the following factors when making decisions regarding children with disabilities and those with special educational needs:

- the views, wishes and feelings of the child or young person, and the child's parents
- the importance of the child or young person, and the child's parents, participating as fully as possible in decisions, and being provided with the information and support necessary to enable participation in those decisions
- the need to support the child or young person, and the child's parents, in order to facilitate the development of the child or young person and to help them achieve the best possible educational outcomes, preparing them effectively for adulthood.

Meeting the needs of children with additional needs within your setting is referred to as *inclusion*. Early Years settings are expected within the legal requirements to organise their provision and resources in ways which enable all children and families to access the Early Years setting. There needs to be a commitment by all Early Years professionals to develop their knowledge and professional skills to be able to understand the ways in which provision can be made inclusive and be able to meet the needs of all children. For some children, who have complex needs and require expert support and care, their needs may have to be met in partnership through a multiagency perspective, including parents being the child's advocate.

THE RIGHTS OF THE CHILD

The United Nations Convention on the Rights of the Child (UNCRC; UN, 1989) is a legally binding international agreement which sets out the civil, political, economic, social and cultural rights of every child, regardless of their race, religion or ability. One of the things the UNCRC does is to make it clear that human rights apply to children and young people as much as they do to adults.

CASE STUDY 14.1

JAMAL

Jamal is four years old and has a diagnosis of autistic spectrum disorder. He has recently started at his local Reception class in a mainstream primary school. He is able to communicate with some spoken language but this is limited. His pronunciation is not clear. The staff within the Reception class help him by using photos or symbols. To be able to support Jamal and thinking about his transition into school, the staff had a meeting and thought about some things which could help him before he started full time.

- They created a photo book with photographs of all the main areas within the nursery.
- They created key times throughout the day – for example, when snack times will take place, lunch time and other significant times – provided by pictures and symbols.
- Jamal was given videos of the key members of staff that he can watch on his iPad.
- Jamal's key worker will visit Jamal at home to find out about the ways in which his family support him and also to show him that they are there to work together.

This case study may sound familiar to a lot of you. Can you think of other ways in which you could support Jamal?

Children and young people don't have as much power as adults: they can't vote, and they don't have as much money. But Article 12 says they still have the human right to have opinions and for these opinions to be heard and taken seriously. It says that the opinions of children and young people should be considered when people make decisions about things that involve them. Their opinions shouldn't be dismissed out of hand on the grounds of age but taken seriously with their evolving capacities taken into account. Article 12 also says children and young people should be given the information they need to make good decisions.

Article 12 is linked to making sure children and young people feel able to express their opinions. It states that they shouldn't feel their opinions will be dismissed or regarded as invalid because of their age. It also makes a bold statement that children and young people need to know about this right so that they can exercise it and that adults need to know about this right, so they don't dismiss it.

QUESTIONS AND ANSWERS

Q1. Does Article 12 of the UNCRC apply to everyone under 18?

A. Yes

The opinion of the child and young person should be considered everywhere, including in their home and early childhood setting. Article 12 applies to everyone, for example:

- special materials should be produced for children and young people with disabilities if they need these to make their views heard. In particular, how are we making use of other communication aids such as Makaton?
- special consideration should be given to children who are from vulnerable situations, such as in care or are refugees;
- care should be taken that voices of all genders are equally listened to.

Q2. Does Article 12 mean that a child always has to give a view?

A. Article 12 doesn't necessarily mean that children have to express an opinion if they don't want to. They have the ability to refuse to give their opinion for any reason. Article 12 shouldn't be used to pressure them into giving it.

Q3. How can Article 12 be put into practice?

A. It is important to be able to tell children and young people about Article 12 and the rights that it gives them.

Practitioners should work in collaboration with parents and carers to think about Article 12. They should be able to find out what stops children and young people from having a say and think about how things can be changed.

THE CHILDREN ACT 2004

The Children Act 2004 requires Early Years and childcare settings to promote anti-discriminatory practice within their work and requires you as a professional working with children to promote 'their needs' with a paramount of importance.

KEY FINDINGS

Since the 2004 Children Act, there has been a substantial improvement in the legal and policy changes for children. These have been focused primarily on education, community and democratic decision-making, as well as collective decision-making.

THE EYFS AND MEETING ALL CHILDREN'S LEARNING AND DEVELOPMENT NEEDS

The main approach within the EYFS recognises that external factors play a huge part in children's learning and development. An inclusive approach should be at the forefront of provision to challenge disadvantage and discrimination.

The Early Years outcomes guidance suggests that practitioners can use non-traditional assessment methods to assess the extent to which children are developing at expected levels for their age based on the statutory Early Years outcomes guidance. At each stage of their learning and development, the guidelines describe what most children do, including seven learning areas:

- communication and language;
- physical development;
- personal, social and emotional development;
- literacy;
- mathematics;
- understanding of the world;
- expressive arts and design.

In the EYFS framework, there is a specific opportunity for providing written assessment when the child reaches the age of two.

PROGRESS CHECK AT AGE TWO

The aims of the progress check at age two include that practitioners should note areas where children are progressing well and identify any areas where progress is less than expected so that they can take action to address developmental concerns, including working within a multiagency context.

It is essential that practitioners develop a targeted plan to support a child with significant emerging concerns (or an identified SEN or disability) by involving other professionals, such as, for example, the setting's SENCO or the area SENCO, as needed. It is important that the summary highlights the following areas:

- good progress is being made;
- some additional support might be needed;
- there is a concern that a child may have a developmental delay (which may indicate SEN or disability).

Under the universal Healthy Child Programme, health visitors assess children's physical development milestones between the ages of two and three. In 2015, it was proposed to introduce an integrated review that would cover the development areas included in the two-year review of the Healthy Child Programme and the two-year progress review of the EYFS. This integrated review would include the following components:

- identify the child's progress, strengths and needs at this age in order to promote positive outcomes in health and wellbeing, learning and development;
- enable appropriate intervention and support for children and their families, where progress is less than expected;
- generate information which can be used to plan services and contribute to the reduction of inequalities in children's outcomes.

GAINING THE VOICE OF THE CHILD

Gaining the voice of the child is integral to key learning and developmental outcomes and CoETL. There are close links to British values, democracy, diversity and equality.

The voice of the child is integral within any assessment practice. Children can be included in thinking about and assessing their own learning and development if this is well structured and supported by the professionals. Children have the right to be listened to and their views are highly valued. Children who speak English as an additional language and those with speech or other developmental delays or disability may not be able to communicate verbally, but they can communicate their interests in other ways, demonstrating their likes and dislikes through gestures, actions, body language, signing or through the medium of drawing and paintings.

Ways of gaining the voice of the child for children who have development or speech delays include:

- Makaton signing;
- drawing/painting;
- role play;
- gestures;
- voice dissatisfaction – through sounds;
- body language.

Gaining the voice of the child should be a daily process within your practice. However, we sometimes take the day-to-day communications that we have with children for granted. We need to step back and listen, observe and take every interaction with children in your care as communication and part of telling, building a story about the child.

EFFECTIVE LISTENING AND COMMUNICATING

It is important that, as professionals in early childhood, we think of continual ways of gaining the voice of the child, not just while they are in settings but holistically too. What I mean by this is having internal and external factors to support the child – for example, parents/carers, family, the environment and their community.

Table 14.1 Ways of gaining the voice of the child

Age of the child	Outcomes of gaining the voice of the child
Pre-birth	• Ensure mother is engaged with midwifery service • Effect of mother's lifestyle on the health and development of the unborn child • Make sure that father, partner of the mother is involved • Extended family members are available to support parents • How does the mother present emotionally and physically? • Are parents preparing for the birth of the child? Take on board home conditions; is hygiene within the home adequate? • Involve the parents in the decision of their child
0–3 years	• Assess the child's basic ability to talk and communicate their feelings. This can also be achieved through observation for younger children and babies • Make questions age-appropriate • Be willing to differentiate activities so that children feel unique and noticed • Observe the child in play – what does this tell you? • Parent and child relationship – what is this telling you? • Any historical perspectives needed to be taken on board • Make use of different mediums to gather the data for the voice for the child • Coordinate and advocate for the child with other agencies where this is needed • With very young children and those with a learning disability, your observations are a big part of representing the voice of the child
3–5 years	• Assess the child's basic ability to talk and communicate their feelings. This can also be achieved through observation for younger children and babies • Make questions age-appropriate • Be willing to differentiate activities so that children feel unique and noticed • Observe the child in play – what does this tell you? • Parent and child relationship – what is this telling you? • Any historical perspectives needed to be taken on board • Make use of different mediums to gather the data for the voice for the child • Coordinate and advocate for the child with other agencies where this is needed • With very young children and those with a learning disability, your observations are a big part of representing the voice of the child • Use visuals and feelings cards/pictures to help the child explain to you the ways they feel • Purchase appropriate materials

WORKING WITH PARENTS

The *Code of Practice* (DfE and DoH, 2015) states that children, parents and carers must be involved actively in assessment and decision-making processes at all stages of the child's development. There is a language or jargon associated with every field of knowledge. Communication with parents may be hindered by the use of a specialist language. It is essential to share any specialised language we are using if we wish to share power equally with our parents. By sharing this technical language with parents, we are also sharing our knowledge of how children learn. The language could be simplified, but parents might find that patronising. If we decide arbitrarily that the language is too difficult for parents to understand, we will find it difficult to claim a desire to be equal partners. Our pedagogy becomes more explicit as soon as we share information about the curriculum, usually during the initial home visit or first session. By providing explanations, we are able to gain a deeper understanding of the concepts.

According to Hunt (2022), parent partnerships are now recognised as being crucial for children's healthy development and for their future successes and are a fundamental central part to the EYFS in England. Just like children are unique, we also need to allow our parents to feel that they come with unique qualities too. Every parent will bring their own set of values, beliefs, attitudes and backgrounds to an Early Years setting. Being aware and fully understanding these factors will give you opportunities to build and engage in a meaningful relationship with them. Borkett (2021) explores the unique aspects of family life in communities and exposes the nature of support that parents need (Borkett, 2018). Taking Brooker's (2016) model, called the *triangle of care*, Borkett explains that hierarchies within Early Years settings need to be dismantled and moved towards a triangle of care, seeing the professional, parent and child as equal (see Figure 14.1).

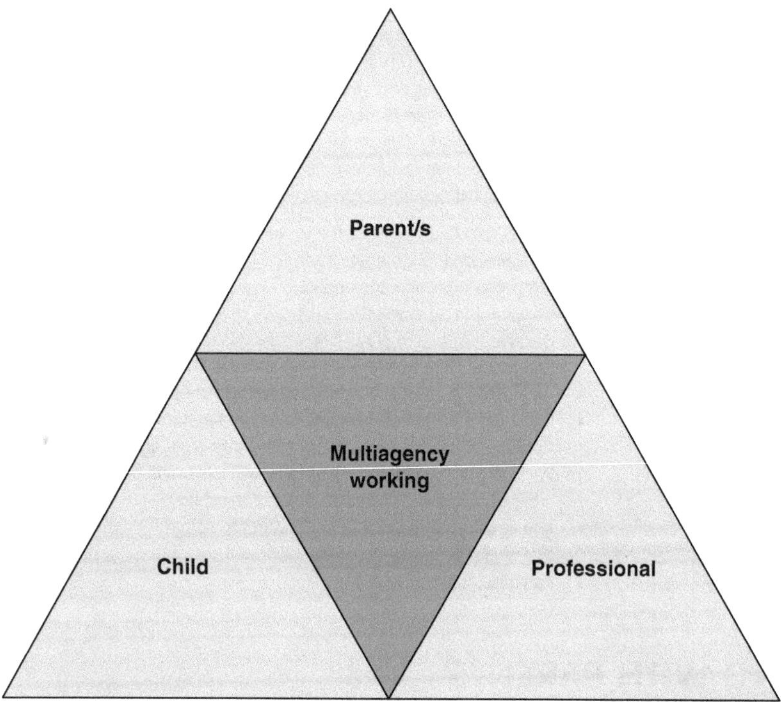

Figure 14.1 The triangle of care

Source: Adapted from Brooker (2016).

However, it is important to remember that when a child has SEND, while the triangle of care is relevant, it should include the significance of other professionals working with the family. So, we have adapted this and placed *multiagency working* in the centre of the triangle. We also want to discuss the model which has been developed by Bradbury and Grimmer (2024), where they discuss the child in the now. Figure 14.2 explores why a sense of belonging focuses on the child *now*, developing a child-centred approach regarding what children need. By focusing on a child's holistic needs, it portrays a positive picture for their learning and positions their wellbeing at the centre of their learning and development. We must not fall into the trap of cramming lost learning to catch up or making children do things when they are not ready to do them, thus placing more pressure on our children; instead we must focus on the *now*. We both believe that this model would be a positive starting point from which to look at how we can best support a child with SEND and focus on creating a positive sense of belonging for them.

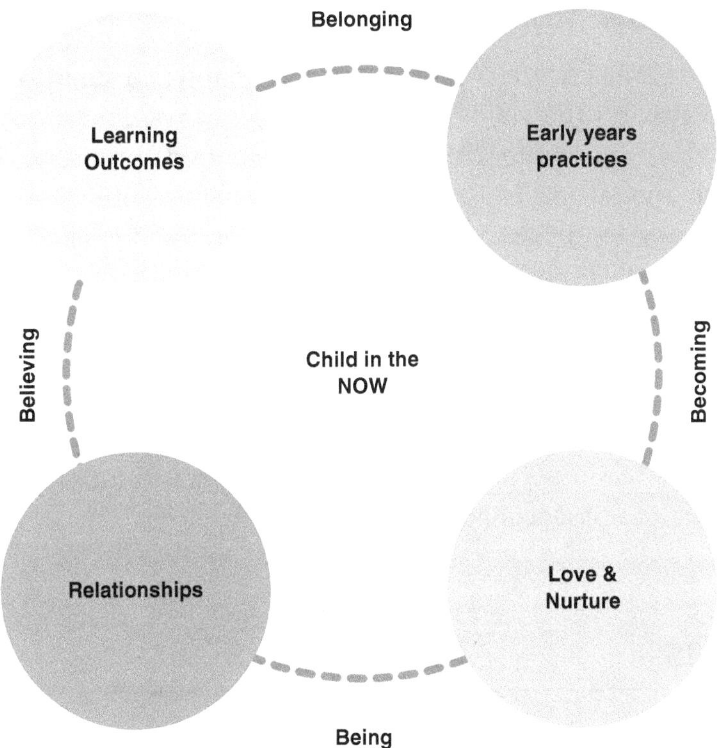

Figure 14.2 The child in the now

Source: Bradbury and Grimmer (2024).

REFLECTION 14.1

1. In what ways can you adopt a loving and nurturing approach with parents and family members to support their child?
2. Think about each child in the *now* that may need some additional support or intervention. Do they feel that they belong? Are their voices being heard? Do you support them becoming and being? How do you demonstrate that you believe in them?
3. Does your setting include holistic approaches for children with SEND such as external workshops for parents and children; how do you keep up to date with making sure that you are aware of services which are needed for children and families?

KEY POINTS OF THE CHAPTER

Unlike other SEND chapters, we wanted this chapter to stand out. Our primary focus was on the child. In this chapter, you will find a narrative that provides a starting point for developing child-centred approaches to support a child with special needs. The child is at the centre of everything we do when it comes to providing learning opportunities for all children. The importance of valuing each and every child cannot be overstated.

A concept highlighted by Bradbury and Grimmer (2024) is the child in the *now*, which emphasises the importance of allowing children the time to develop rather than focusing on catching up with them. It has been realised that, for some children, a catch-up narrative may be more harmful than beneficial. In order to support a child with SEND, in fact to support all children, it is necessary to utilise a child-centred approach.

REFERENCES

Borkett, P. (2018) *Cultural Diversity and Inclusion in the Early Years Education*. London: Routledge.

Borkett, P. (2021) *Special Educational Needs in the Early Years: A Guide to Inclusive Practice*. London: Sage.

Bradbury, A. and Grimmer, T. (2024) *Love and Nurture in the Early Years*. London: Learning Matters.

Brooker, L. (2016) Childminders, parents and policy: Testing the triangle of care. *Journal of Early Childhood Research*, 14(1), 69–83.

Department for Education (DfE) (2024) *Early Years Foundation Stage (EYFS) Statutory Framework*. Available at: www.gov.uk/government/publications/early-years-foundation-stage-framework--2 [Accessed 1 April 2024].

DfE and Department of Health (DoH) (2015) *Special Educational Needs and Disability Code of Practice: 0 to 25 Years*. Available at: www.gov.uk/government/publications/send-code-of-practice-0-to-25 [Accessed 1 December 2023].

Grimmer, T. (2021) *Developing a Loving Pedagogy in the Early Years: How Love Fits with Professional Practice*. London: Routledge.

Hunt, M. (2022) *Helping Every Child to Thrive in the Early Years: How to Overcome the Effect of Disadvantage*. London: Routledge.

United Nations (UN) (1989) *United Nations Convention on the Rights of the Child (UNCRC)*. Available at: www.unicef.org.uk/wp-content/uploads/2016/08/unicef-convention-rights-child-uncrc.pdf [Accessed 31 May 2024].

INDEX

Page numbers followed by "f" indicate figures; those followed by "t" indicate tables.

Zeitfracht Medien GmbH
Ferdinand-Jühlke-Straße 7
99095 Erfurt, Deutschland
produktsicherheit@kolibri360.de